THE JEWISH THOUGHT AND PSYCHOANALYSIS LECTURES

THE JEWISH THOUGHT AND PSYCHOANALYSIS LECTURES

Edited by

Harvey Schwartz

PHOENIX
PUBLISHING HOUSE
firing the mind

First published in 2020 by
Phoenix Publishing House Ltd
62 Bucknell Road
Bicester
Oxfordshire OX26 2DS

British Library Cataloguing in Publication Data

A C.I.P. for this book is available from the British Library

ISBN-13: 978-1-912691-23-4

Typeset by Medlar Publishing Solutions Pvt Ltd, India

www.firingthemind.com

For Jan and Eric
and
Gary and Steve

"*The vast majority of the words of the sages are meant in a metaphorical and allegorical way ... therefore, don't be alarmed when you see words which appear foolish and distant from wisdom ... they are really hidden messages which are very profound and intelligent.*"

Be'eir haGolah *(1598)*
Judah Loew ben Bezalel (The Maharal)

"*In short what according to the opinion of other authors [on dreams] is supposed to be merely an arbitrary improvisation hurriedly brought together in the embarrassment of the moment, this we treat as a holy text.*"

The Interpretation of Dreams *(1900)*
Sigmund Freud

Contents

About the editor and contributors

Ruth Calderon, PhD, a former Member of Knesset from the Yesh Atid party and Deputy Speaker of the Knesset (2013–2015), is an educator and academic Talmud scholar. In 1989 she established the Elul pluralistic beit midrash. In 1996 she founded Alma, the Home for Hebrew Culture. She served as the head of the Culture and Education Department at the National Library and as a faculty member of the Mandel Leadership Institute. She received her MA and PhD in Talmud from the Hebrew University. She is a graduate of the first cohort of the Mandel School for Educational Leadership. In recognition of her work, she received the AVI CHAI Prize for Jewish Education, the Rothberg Prize in Jewish Education, and several honorary doctorates.

Stephen Frosh, PhD, is professor in the Department of Psychosocial Studies (which he founded) at Birkbeck, University of London. He has a background in academic and clinical psychology and was consultant clinical psychologist at the Tavistock Clinic, London, throughout the 1990s, specializing in family and individual psychotherapy with children and young people. He is a fellow of the Academy of Social Sciences, an academic associate of the British Psychoanalytical Society, a founding member of the Association of Psychosocial Studies, and an honorary member of the Institute of Group Analysis.

Stephen Frosh is the author of many books and papers on psychosocial studies and on psychoanalysis. His books include *Hauntings: Psychoanalysis and Ghostly Transmissions*; *Feelings*; *A Brief Introduction to Psychoanalytic Theory*; *Psychoanalysis Outside the Clinic*; and *Hate and the Jewish Science: Anti-Semitism, Nazism and Psychoanalysis*. His most recent book is *Simply Freud* (Simply Charly, 2018). His current research interests are in processes of acknowledgment and recognition after social violence and in questions of social and ethnic identity. A book on this topic, *Those Who Come After*, was published by Palgrave Macmillan in 2019.

Sander L. Gilman, PhD, is a distinguished professor of the Liberal Arts and Sciences as well as professor of psychiatry at Emory University. A cultural and literary historian, he is the author or editor of more than ninety books, the last his *Stand Up Straight! A History of Posture* (Reaktion Press, 2018). His most recent edited volume is *Jews on the Move: Modern Cosmopolitanist Thought and Its Others*, published in 2018 by Routledge. He is the author of the basic study of the visual stereotyping of the mentally ill, *Seeing the Insane*, published by John Wiley and Sons in 1982 (reprinted 1996 and 2014), as well as the standard study of *Jewish Self-Hatred*, the title of his Johns Hopkins University Press monograph of 1986, which is still in print. He has been a visiting professor at numerous universities in North America, South Africa, the United Kingdom, Germany, Israel, China, and New Zealand. He was president of the Modern Language Association in 1995. He has been awarded a doctor of laws (honoris causa) at the University of Toronto in 1997, elected an honorary professor of the Free University in Berlin (2000), an honorary member of the American Psychoanalytic Association (2007), and made a fellow of the American Academy of Arts and Sciences (2016).

Marsha Aileen Hewitt, PhD, is a professor in the Department for the Study of Religion at the University of Toronto, and the Faculty of Divinity at Trinity College. She teaches undergraduate and graduate courses in psychoanalytic theory and clinical practice, psychoanalytic psychology of religion, critical theory, and method and theory in the study of religion. Her most recent publications include *Freud on Religion* (2014), "Christian Anti-Judaism and Early Object Relations Theory" (2018), "The Psychoanalytic Occult in Freud and Contemporary Theory" (2017), and "Spirits in the Mind, Gods in the Brain: Contemporary Psychologies of Religious

Experience" (2016). Her latest book, *Legacies of the Occult: Psychoanalysis, Religion and Unconscious Communication* is forthcoming. Her current project is *A Psychoanalytic Psychology of Religion: Possession, Trances and Transference.*

Marsha Hewitt is a psychoanalyst in private practice, and a supervisor and faculty member at the Toronto Institute for Contemporary Psychoanalysis.

Eran J. Rolnik, MD, PhD, is a training and supervising analyst, Israel Psychoanalytic Society (IPA) member, psychiatrist and historian. He has been the translator and scientific editor of numerous volumes of Freud's essays; author of *Freud in Zion: Psychoanalysis and the Making of Modern Jewish Identity* (Karnac, 2012), and coeditor of *Einstein, Freud and the Wars to Come* (Carmel, Jerusalem, 2018). His recent book, *Sigmund Freud—Letters* (Modan, 2019) is an annotated collection of Freud's letters to seventy different recipients.

Harvey Schwartz, MD, is a training and supervising analyst at the Psychoanalytic Association of New York (PANY) and the Psychoanalytic Center of Philadelphia (PCOP). He is a clinical professor of psychiatry and human behavior at the Sidney Kimmel Medical School, Thomas Jefferson University in Philadelphia, where he is in the private practice of psychoanalysis and psychotherapy. He is the founder and executive producer of the IPA Podcast *Psychoanalysis On and Off the Couch*, and he is the founder of the *Jewish Thought and Psychoanalysis* website and lecture series.

Eli Zaretsky, PhD, is professor of history at the New School for Social Research, New York City. He is the author of *Political Freud, Secrets of the Soul: A Social and Cultural History of Psychoanalysis,* and *Capitalism, the Family and Personal Life.*

Preface

Freud's relationship with his Judaism—his by virtue of his self-description as a "fanatical Jew"—was framed by two of his convictions. He was centered both by his passionate cultural affiliation and by his atheism. Within these internal guideposts lay a Jewish life layered by tensions, pleasures, and identifications. His creation, psychoanalysis, has labored to honor its Jewish influences. Recent studies of these insights have contributed to the current clinical interest in more carefully listening to the individual meanings of analysands' religious life.

The lecture series from which this book evolved was designed to introduce to the public both the similarities and the differences between the psychoanalytic and the Jewish world views. The lectures began in 2013 in a synagogue in downtown Philadelphia. The audiences for these lectures reflected a mix of varied interests. Psychoanalytic colleagues as well as other mental health professionals joined with synagogue members along with other urban and suburban Philadelphians.

The theme of each presentation was to consider an aspect of the Jewishness of psychoanalysis. The topics covered included Freud's own relation with his cultural identification, the times in which he and his circle of fellow clinicians lived, the similarities and differences between a religious and an analytic way of experiencing oneself, the impact of anti-Semitism on their work and their lives, and the dynamism of psychoanalysis in the

State of Israel. My introductions to the presentations have been kept in their spoken format as introductions to the chapters of this book. The chapters themselves have been edited by the authors to read more formally. The conversational format of my engagement with Ruth Calderon has been maintained and is presented verbatim.

A secondary intention of this lecture series was to make overt what has long been latent. The historically high percentage of psychoanalysts who have been Jewish is both well known and unspoken. That there are many reasons for both of these phenomena goes without saying. The purpose of this text, like clinical work in the office, is to bring to light that the fears we associate with speaking freely of such matters need not limit us. Curiosity, not to mention pride, in one's cultural affiliation invites others to feel the same about their own heritages. Irish, Italian, Indian analysts all bring their own cultural character to this work. We will enrich each other by acknowledging the idiosyncrasies of our lives and their impact on our work.

I wish to thank the contributors to this text. They are among the thought leaders of our generation who work at the interface of the intrapsychic and religious states of mind. We can learn how each has influenced the other and perhaps how each has been enriched by the other. Their scholarship is remarkable, and we are all wiser for studying it.

I would like to express my appreciation to the administrative staff at Beth Zion—Beth Israel synagogue in Philadelphia, the venue for these lectures. Special thanks to Terri Soifer, Tovah Rosenthal, Arlene Fickler, and Rabbis Ira Stone and Abraham Friedman.

I would also like to acknowledge my colleagues in the Psychoanalytic Study Group of Philadelphia who share with me a love for this work.

I also wish to acknowledge my wife who has supported this project for the past six years and has continued to be an inspiration for my personal and professional development.

Harvey Schwartz, MD
Philadelphia

CHAPTER ONE

Insight and tradition: the Enlightenment, psychoanalysis, and the Jews*

Eli Zaretsky

Introduction

On the occasion of his seventy-fifth birthday on May 6, 1931, Freud received birthday greetings from the Chief Rabbi of Vienna, Rabbi David Feuchtwang. In response to those greetings he wrote back to the rabbi, "In some place in my soul in a very hidden corner I am a fanatical Jew. I'm very much astonished to discover myself as such in spite of all efforts to be unprejudiced and impartial. What can I do against my age?" (Hes, 1986, p. 322). How do we understand what it meant for Freud to feel that he was a fanatical Jew? Furthermore, how do we understand what it meant for any seventy-five-year-old man in 1931 Vienna to feel that he was a fanatical Jew? For our purposes what does it matter what kind of Jew Freud felt himself to be? He was an atheist but a proud cultural Jew. Does Freud's relation to his Jewishness really influence our thinking about whether there is or isn't a relation between psychoanalytic thinking and Jewish thinking? The all too easy analogy would be with Einstein. Would we care what kind of Jew Einstein felt himself to be in trying to understand

---

*A version of this chapter was previously published in a somewhat different form as "In the Shadow of the Holocaust" in *Political Freud: A History* (2015) by Eli Zaretsky, published by Columbia University Press. Reproduced with permission.

his contribution to science and to the world? I think we approach them differently. If we boil the question down—is there something Jewish about psychoanalysis—distant cousins or strangers? Being true both to a Jewish and a psychoanalytic way of thinking, as you might imagine, we are not going to get instant answers to those questions. We are going to get more questions but hopefully these questions will be more nuanced, more historically based, and, most importantly, will begin to take the unspoken issue which is common in the community—that there is some overlap between Jewish thinking and psychoanalytic thinking and have it be a topic of conversation. This way we can transform it from the latent issue that it often is and instead have it be a topic for us to talk about both now and in the future.

First, a bit about Freud. Freud was born on May 6, 1856, the year they finished the construction of the Academy of Music here in Philadelphia. He was born in a small town in what is now the Czech Republic. His parents were from a long line of Orthodox and Hassidic rabbis. They moved the family to Vienna when he was four and by most accounts, though not all, his family then dropped all religious rituals and observances. Freud was raised heavily influenced by the Enlightenment of the time and he became a precocious student. He was schooled privately by a rabbi but later repeatedly claimed no knowledge of Hebrew.

The cultural environment within which he grew was on the one hand characterized by the intellectual freedoms of the burgeoning modern era. Simultaneously he found himself caged in by the insistent otherness of growing anti-Semitism. He decidedly did not choose to ease his path through the route of conversion as many others of his generation did. "I was a Jew and it always appeared to me not only undignified but outright foolish to deny it" (E. L. Freud, 1961, pp. 367–368). Sigmund Freud surrounded himself with Jews, most of his friends were Jews, most of his colleagues were Jews, and most of his early patients were Jews. In search of a supportive community of like-minded secular Jews he sought out the B'nai B'rith. Commenting in 1926 on his loneliness before joining the B'nai B'rith he wrote them,

> This isolation aroused in me the longing for a circle of excellent men with high ideals who would accept me in friendship despite my temerity. That you were Jews could only be welcome to me. I find the attraction of Judaism and the Jews to be irresistible. And before

long there followed the realization that it was only to my Jewish
nature that I owed the two qualities that have become indispensable
to me throughout my difficult life. Because I was a Jew I found myself
free of many prejudices which restrict others in the use of the intellect. In addition as a Jew I was prepared to be in the opposition and
to renounce agreement with the compact majority. (ibid.)

As ferocious as Freud was in proclaiming his cultural pride, so too was he
equally committed to protecting his young child of psychoanalysis from the
dangers it faced in its hostile environment. He feared that given its Jewish
birthright it would be dismissed as degenerate and disregarded, outlawed,
and most importantly, misunderstood. He feared it being characterized as a
mere "Jewish science." His remedy was to find a gentile leader who would
talisman-like be able to protect it from the attacks of the anti-Semites
and represent it as a universally applicable set of discoveries. He chose
Carl Jung, a Swiss psychiatrist and a pastor's son. Eventually their relationship and their understandings of how the mind worked led them their
separate ways.

For our purposes it's worth taking note that the very gentile-ness that
Freud sought in Jung led him also to conclude that as we say in today's
language, "he just didn't get it." He wrote about his difficulty with Jung to
his close Jewish colleague in Berlin, Karl Abraham:

> Please be tolerant and do not forget that it is really easier for you
> than it is for Jung to follow my ideas, for in the first place you are
> completely independent, and you are closer to my intellectual con-
> stitution because of racial kinship, while he as a Christian pastor's
> son finds his way to me only against great inner resistances. His asso-
> ciation with us is more valuable for that. I nearly said that it was only
> by his appearance on the scene that psycho-analysis escaped the
> danger of becoming a Jewish national affair. (H. C. Abraham & E. L.
> Freud, 1966)

It appears that at least at that time Freud associated a Jewish mind with
a facile psychoanalytic mind. That is our question. Do we really think
there is something Jewish about psychoanalysis? Stephen Frosh, a British
psychoanalytic scholar, has approached this question and responded in
this way,

Relentlessly interior and self-reflexive Jewish thought continually examines and interprets playfully sometimes, with anguish at others. This too is part of the psychoanalytic response to the terrors and thrills of modernity. Freud claimed that his Jewish identity freed him from restrictions of the intellect and in the end, he was grateful for it whatever the costs. The crucial point is that just as post emancipation Jewish identity is built on the knife edged awareness of the potential and dangers of the modern experience so is psychoanalysis. Each informs the other. Each is the product of the same underlying socio historical process. (2005, p. 31; see also Chapter 2)

To return to the original fear Freud had about his work being derogated as a mere "Jewish science," in 1978 Anna Freud was invited to deliver the inaugural lecture for the Sigmund Freud Chair at Hebrew University in Jerusalem. As part of her speech she referenced the Jewish science question:

During the era of its existence, psychoanalysis has entered into connection with various academic institutions, not always with satisfactory results. It has also, repeatedly, experienced rejection by them, been criticized for its methods being imprecise, its findings not open to proof by experiment, for being unscientific, even for being a "Jewish science". However the other derogatory comments may be evaluated, it is, I believe, the last-mentioned connotation which, under present circumstances, can serve as a title of honor. (1978, pp. 145–148)

Last summer my wife and I traveled to Berlin. We visited many Holocaust related monuments. The one that made the largest impression on us was perhaps the smallest. Picture this—there is a courtyard and it's surrounded by apartment buildings all around it. There's a grassy area in the middle of it. And in the middle of that courtyard is a table—a simple table and two chairs. One of the chairs is standing upright in relation to the table and the other chair is lying on its back. The inclination is to go pick up the chair, to right the chair, to fix it. It's askew. There's something wrong here and it's unsettling. One goes over to the chair and you feel that it is stuck. Nevertheless, you try to pick it up and you can't. You can't change the chair that is stuck on its back.

This monument marks the historical event that took place in that courtyard, and in many other courtyards. It's called *Der Verlassene Raum* (The Deserted Room).

In this courtyard lived a number of Jewish families. During the War the Nazis would come in to the apartments and would interrupt the meal. They would tear the family away from the meal—would tear the family away from the table and would tear the family away from their lives. But it didn't stop there. What then often happened was that the non-Jewish neighbors would walk into that same apartment, would sit down at that same table. They would pick up the chair, they would straighten the table cloth and they would finish the soup. They would take over the apartment as their own. As if what happened didn't happen. As if this assault never took place. The chair was picked up.

Similarly, as Freud and Zaretsky and others have pointed out, our biblical Moses went to the mountaintop to find, declare, and experience a monotheistic God—a gift he felt he would give to his people. This God was to be of a different sort. It was to be a God that one could not touch, one could not see. The experience of this God was meant to elevate one from what was otherwise a mere sensual experience to something different, something more challenging to consider. Moses came down the mountain and he saw that his people were having a tough time of it. When they were being faced with frustration, disappointment, and uncertainty they turned to the familiar—to the shiny. They turned to gold. They turned to idols that they could touch. The ethereal abstracted God was beyond them at that moment.

Similarly, for those of us who have had the good fortune to be patients in psychoanalysis, for those of us who have the added good fortune to be able to conduct psychoanalyses, for all us humans, there comes a time when something is stirring within us. Something is bubbling up inside us. It could be hurt. It could be anger. It could be tenderness. It could be lust. It could be a tear. Without even knowing it we turn away from it. We find something with which to distract ourselves. We pick up the chair that is unsettling to us. We find some gold to distract ourselves. We seek something pretty with which to preoccupy ourselves to turn away from a disturbing internal emotional truth.

When all goes well in the psychoanalysis, the analyst and analysand will work together at those moments and recognize and discover that the intolerance for that truth at that moment isn't necessary. It isn't truly based on adult thinking and functioning. We come to recognize that the notion that we can't feel and know this truth is in fact defined and limited by our childhood way of thinking. We can discover that we can be free from these outdated limitations to our honesty and creativity.

For me, whether understanding Freud, Moses, or post-Holocaust modernity, what the truth of these topics has in common is that they challenge us to engage them with our deepest authenticity. The unpleasant truths of our past, our Gods, and our history deserve nothing less.

Harvey Schwartz

* * *

Of the enduring books of the twentieth century, *Moses and Monotheism* remains one of the most difficult to interpret. Written while Freud was old, sick, and in the shadow of the Nazi terror, based on scant historical research, the book (1939a) describes Moses as an Egyptian and the Jews as the bearers of an "archaic heritage" that includes their collective, unconscious memory of murdering Moses. But while the book has spawned endless controversy, nearly all commentators agree that its subject is Jewish identity. Writing in the wake of the Holocaust, the earliest interpreters, such as Gershom Scholem, Leo Strauss, and Paul Ricoeur criticized the book for denying the Jewish people their national ideals. After a long hiatus, interest in the book revived when Jacques Derrida and Yosef Hayim Yerushalmi described it as "a psychological document of Freud's inner life," focused on Freud's own Judaism. Most recently Edward Said, representing a third, "postcolonial" generation, praised Freud's conviction that Moses was an Egyptian for demonstrating that no identity can "constitute or even imagine itself without [a] radical originary break or flaw which will not be repressed."

Freud himself reinforced the view that the book essentially concerns Jewish identity. He wrote to Arnold Zweig in September 1934 that the subject of the book was "what has really created the particular character of the Jew" and how has the Jew "in view of the renewed persecutions … drawn upon himself this undying hatred?" (Kurzweil, 1989, p. 293). But at a deeper and perhaps largely unconscious level the driving force behind the book was Freud's worry concerning the survival of psychoanalysis. Writing the book while dying, and in the course of being driven into exile, Freud was well aware that psychoanalysis could be stamped out just as quickly and surprisingly as monotheism had been stamped out in ancient Egypt. For Freud the survival of the values he associated with the discovery of the unconscious was far more important than the survival of the Jewish religion, which he considered of little value, and even of Jewish ethnicity, to which he was deeply attached, although differently from the way he was attached to psychoanalysis. Of course, it must be said that Freud, like everyone else, had no idea that he was facing the attempted destruction of the Jewish people, a fact we know now that has profoundly shaped our perceptions (see Zaretsky, 2012).

Furthermore, Freud didn't consider the question of the survival of psychoanalysis alone but posed the question of the survival of spiritual or intellectual advances in general. For that reason, the book should be read as a meditation on the overall crisis of the Western world in the light of the rise of Nazism, comparable to contemporaneous works, also largely written in exile, such as Erich Auerbach's *Mimesis*, Erwin Panofsky's work on perspective, and Hans Baron's *Crisis of the Italian Renaissance*. Nazism demonstrated, as perhaps no other current of the twentieth century did, why something like Freud's hypothesis of the unconscious was necessary. That so horrific and primitive an example of sustained hate and destructiveness could arise in the country of Bach and Goethe showed how deluded our sense of ourselves as progressive and enlightened could be. Freud's idea of the unconscious, implicitly defended in *Moses and Monotheism*, is analogous to Auerbach's idea of realism, Panofsky's idea of perspective, or Baron's idea of civic humanism: a tentative and fragile advance in our understanding of subjectivity. In posing the question of the survival of psychoanalysis, Freud joined a group of scholars and thinkers concerned with the question of the survival of core human values overall.

Nor did Freud restrict himself to the thought that the discovery of the unconscious could be wiped out by brutality and violence—it already had been in Germany and Austria while he was writing the book! In addition, Freud feared disintegration from within, as had occurred in ancient tribal societies such as the Hebrews, among whom an unparalleled spiritual breakthrough degenerated into empty ritual and legalism, and in Christianity, where monotheism disintegrated into a cult of martyrs and saints. Analogously, Freud feared that in the United States, where analysis had sparked a pullulating therapeutic industry and become integral to advertising, film, and mass culture, the "gold" of psychoanalysis was being lost in the "dross" of adaptations. For Freud, Judaic monotheism had an *affinity* with psychoanalysis, not in the sense that Freud incorporated "Jewish ideas" into analysis, but in the sense that both were difficult and even ascetic practices subject to vulgarization and distortion as they took a popular form.

What monotheism and psychoanalysis had in common Freud called *Geistigkeit*. Often translated as intellectuality or spirituality, the best English equivalent for *Geistigkeit* may be inwardness or subjectivity. Freud believed that the invention of monotheism had been a world-historical event, not because it created the Hebrew people, but rather because of the prohibition on graven images, which forced the Hebrews into envisioning a God they could not see or feel or touch. For Freud, *Geistigkeit* was a difficult human achievement, which went against the instinctive drive for sensory satisfaction as well as against the mind's unconscious propensity to relive libidinal satisfactions from infancy. *Geistigkeit* was related to the ancient Hebrew idea of holiness (*kedushah*), but it was also related to the German idealist philosophical tradition that had taken shape as a critical response to Anglo-American empiricism and that informed Freud's education and scientific milieu.

In both meanings—spiritual and philosophical—*Geistigkeit* was integral to the idea of the unconscious. Just as the Hebrews could not represent God, and just as Kant could not empirically demonstrate the transcendental subject he hypothesized, so Freud could only infer, not demonstrate, the existence of unconscious mental processes.[1]

The sense in which *Moses and Monotheism* is centered on the survival of the idea of the unconscious will be apparent when we summarize the book's argument. One man, Freud tells us, created Judaism: Moses. He did so by choosing a circle of followers and initiating them into a difficult practice based on instinctual renunciation rather than sensory gratification. His followers, after some enthusiasm, rejected his practice as too demanding, effectively returning to the idol worship from which Moses had rescued them. Eventually his followers killed Moses, and a debased Judaism triumphed. Nonetheless, the repressed memory of Moses' ascetic doctrine survived and was rediscovered centuries later by the prophets.

Now let us make the obvious substitutions. One man created psychoanalysis: Sigmund Freud. He did so by choosing a circle of followers and initiating them into a difficult practice based on instinctual renunciation rather than sensory gratification. His followers, after some enthusiasm, rejected his practice as too demanding, returning to the idol worship from which Freud had rescued them. Eventually his followers killed Freud and a debased psychoanalysis triumphed. Nonetheless, the repressed memory of Freud's ascetic doctrine survived, and its secrets too would be rediscovered centuries later.

Moses and Monotheism, then, should be read in two different but complementary ways. If, at one level, Freud was using psychoanalysis to illuminate the history of Judaism, at another he was using the history of Judaism to illuminate the history of psychoanalysis. Let us start with the latter. Freud's conception of Jewish history has an underlying narrative structure that consists in five parts. In the first the Jews are presented with the monotheistic idea of God, which affords freedom from subordination to the senses and in that way deepens the inner world of the Hebrews; in the second they experience a sense of chosen-ness, of possessing a special treasure that raises them above those who are still immured in sensory and empirical knowledge; in the third they struggle with guilt at not being able to live up to the new ethical ideals associated with having a conscience and being a chosen people; in the fourth they are tempted to abandon their difficult standards and revert to the sensuous polytheism of the Egyptians as well as to the mother gods of the ancient Near East; and in the fifth they rediscover the original monotheistic message. In what follows I will identify five analogous stages in the history of psychoanalysis, stages that also reflect the extent to which psychoanalysis was the product of Jewish history. In a conclusion I return to situate *Moses and Monotheism* in the context of World War II and ask what light it sheds on the place that Judaism and anti-Semitism occupied in that war.

Stage one: the Hebrew God, the unconscious, and the father complex

In all religions, Freud believed, as in all delusions, there was invariably a bit of historical truth. The historical truth behind Judaism, he speculated, was the destruction of the monotheistic cult at the court of Ikhnaton. When Moses, an Egyptian prince or high court official fearing persecution, fled the court and came to the Jews with the message of a single God, the message had terrific force because it was a repetition. It reminded the Jews of the archaic age during which they had been under the spell of the primal father. In *Totem and Taboo* (1912–13) Freud described the murder of the primal father as a single event, but in *Moses and Monotheism* (1939a) he essentially apologized for this, writing "[T]he story is told in a very condensed way, as if what in reality took centuries to achieve, and during that long time was repeated innumerably, had only happened once." Because Moses was himself a great patriarchal figure, he reminded the Hebrews of the primal father, and they found his presence dangerous and unsettling. The Jewish murder of Moses, then, *repeated* the primal slaying of the father, thereby intensifying a preexisting sense of guilt.

The monotheistic message was also a repetition in a second sense, this time of the cultural advance that occurred in the murder's wake. Egypt's earlier religions were polytheistic and oriented toward nature gods. They abounded in pictorial and symbolic representations of spiritual entities and promised life after death. In the monotheism developed at the court of Ikhnaton, by contrast, "all myth, magic and sorcery" were excluded. Instead of the pyramid and the falcon of the earlier Egyptian religion, the sun god was symbolized by "a round disc from which emanate rays terminating in human hands," a symbol Freud called "almost rational." Strikingly, the new religion had no mention of life after death. Of special importance, for Freud, was the *Bilderverbot*, the prohibition on graven images of the deity. The injunction against visualizing or otherwise representing God, he believed, forced a leap from the material and sensual world to the conceptual or intelligible. In Freud's words, "Ideas, memories, and inferences became decisive in contrast to the lower psychical activity which had direct perceptions by the sense organs as its content." This shift from sensory knowledge to conceptual thought, in Freud's view, was an instinctual renunciation, by which Freud meant sublimation, not repression. As such it brought about a rise in self-esteem.

Freud's account of the birth of monotheism parallels the birth of psychoanalysis. Sigmund Freud's father Jacob Freud came from a Hasidic community in Galicia, and at an early age Freud was made familiar with the family Bible. As Freud later wrote, "My deep engrossment in the Bible story (almost as soon as I had learnt the art of reading) had, as I recognized much later, an enduring effect upon the direction of my interest." A patriarchal God and a foundational crime against that God were central to the book of Genesis. In the 1890s, when Freud was developing psychoanalysis, he grappled continually with the question of paternal authority. Although Freud interpreted a dream of his own for the first time in July 1895 and wrote out a draft of *The Interpretation of Dreams*, he could not complete the book for three more years. He explained the delay as the result of his "self-analysis," the introspection and mourning precipitated by his father's death.

The death uprooted him, awakening his past and prompting him to surmise that the death of the father was invariably the most significant event in men's lives. The process of completing *The Interpretation of Dreams* (1900a) and of coming to grips with his father's death went on together. The parts of the book Freud had difficulty finishing were his debts to his predecessors and the formulation of his most original idea, the primary process or unconscious.

For Freud, the formulation of the idea of the unconscious was not the result of an empirical discovery but of a conceptual breakthrough. Blocked from access to consciousness by what Freud was at that point calling the censor, neither the form nor the content of the unconscious could be directly represented. Rather, Freud would free associate to each of his dream fragments, then interpret his associations, and only after interpretation would he *infer* the contents of his unconscious. The proper starting point for analytic introspection, therefore, was the recognition that one *could not know directly* but rather had to infer the contents of one's mind. In this regard Freud echoed Kant, "Just as Kant warned us not to overlook the fact that our perception … must not be regarded as identical with the phenomena perceived but never really discerned, so psychoanalysis bids us not to set conscious perception [that is, our conscious thoughts] in the place of the unconscious mental process which is [their] object" (1915e, p. 171).

To be sure, the Hebrew sense of the sacred and unapproachable—all that is connoted by the Hebrew term *kedushah*—and the Greek discovery of philosophy, mathematics, and of a conceptually grounded science, are very different (Bultmann, 1956). But they have in common a turn toward the inner life, whether seen as spiritual, intellectual, or both, and the Greek and Hebrew strands were mingled in the Hellenistic, Roman, and early Christian eras, becoming part of a common thread of Western civilization. Freud's education had been "neo-Kantian," meaning that the innate or a priori categories of the mind posited by Kant were being redefined as evolutionary products. In a deep sense, however, Freud inflected the Kantian and neo-Kantian thought in which he had been trained with the ancient Hebrew connotations of *kedushah*. The unconscious, as Freud envisioned it, is not merely unknowable as the metaphysical world is, meaning not directly accessible to the senses; it is unknowable because that is where the dead parents, the memories of childhood, including the unconscious memory of the primal murder, lie not wholly buried.[2] Thus, although Freud described the theory of the unconscious as "an extension of the corrections begun by Kant," Freud's core conception around 1900 was that of repression, a concept unknown to Kant and the ultimate source of the dream images that kept the memories of childhood buried. When Freud insisted in *The Interpretation of Dreams* that the *Ur*-image—the dream—be turned into words, he promulgated a new *Bilderverbot*. Freud's insistence—the so-called single rule in psychoanalysis, namely to free associate—bespeaks his identification with Moses. Moses emancipated the Jews from the graven images of Egypt; Freud may have seen himself as emancipating humanity from dream images, opening up not the unconscious but the *repressed* unconscious, the incestuous and murderous wishes of infancy.

Like Moses, Freud needed to share his discovery, a need that initiates stage two in our history. As he formulated the idea of the unconscious, he drew closer to the Jewish community, effectively "choosing" his followers from among them. After returning from Paris in 1885, he had begun working as a private doctor for nervous diseases, primarily with Jewish and immigrant patients. Defiantly opening his first office on Easter Sunday, he presented himself as a convert to the "French" school, often a code word in Vienna for Jewish. He delivered a paper, "On Male Hysteria," supposedly a Jewish disease, before the Viennese Society of Physicians. As anti-capitalist and anti-Semitic feeling mounted in late nineteenth-century Vienna, only the emperor prevented the seating of the populist and anti-Semitic Karl Lueger as mayor, and that only until 1897 (Boyer, 1978, pp. 91–99). Freud responded to Lueger's ascent, as well as to the Dreyfus affair, by joining B'nai B'rith (he remained a member until 1902). In so doing he stepped down the social ladder from the medical and academic intelligentsia to a stratum of ordinary Jewish doctors and businessmen who, "if they could not assist or further his scientific pursuits, did not threaten or discourage him" (Schorske, 1981, p. 186). It was from this relatively meager stratum of self-employed Jewish doctors that Freud "chose" his earliest followers.

Among these followers, Freud became a father figure himself, someone—as he wrote of Moses—"in whom one of the human impulses has found its strongest and purest, and therefore often its most one-sided, expression," although the impulse for which he stood was subjectivity and rational thought rather than monotheism. Like Moses, Freud eventually became a great cultural superego, a whole "climate of opinion," as Auden wrote in a wonderful poem (1940). Like the Moses of Freud's imagination, many of Freud's followers sought to slay him, at least figuratively. But, unlike Moses,

Freud sought to thwart his detractors by telling his own story—in *Moses and Monotheism*. Thus the first stage in the history of psychoanalysis, the founding, was embedded with Judaic meanings, and so later Freud was able to tell the history of the Jews in a way that illuminated the first stage in the history of analysis.

Stage two: narcissism and the chosen people

When the British Zionist analyst David Eder died in 1936, Freud recalled their meeting decades earlier: "We were both Jews and knew of each other that we carried in us that miraculous thing in common which, inaccessible to any analysis so far, makes the Jew." Through writing *Moses and Monotheism*, Freud believed he had discovered the origins of the "miraculous thing" that Jews have in common. It was their "secret treasure," their intellectuality, which gave them their self-confidence and sense of superiority in regard to pagan cultures that had remained "under the spell of sensuality" (1939a, pp. 115, 118). Characteristically, Freud traced this "miraculous" feeling to the Hebrew people's childlike relation to Moses. He wrote,

> The conception of a god suddenly "choosing" a people, making it "his" people and himself its own god is astonishing.... I believe it is the only case in the history of human religions. In other cases the people and their god belong inseparably together; they are one from the beginning. Sometimes, it is true, we hear of a people adopting another god, but never of a god choosing a new people. Perhaps we approach an understanding of this unique happening when we reflect on the connection between Moses and the Jewish people. Moses had stooped to the Jews, had made them his people; they were his "chosen people". (1939a, p. 45)

Being chosen was not without difficulties. When Moses presented the idea of one god to the Hebrew people, they seized upon it because it was a revival of the earlier submission to the primal father. But they also seized upon monotheism because it reproduced the gain made when, after the murder of the father, the brothers renounced their aggression and founded law, ethics, and religion. Like those who accomplished the first advances of civilization, the early Hebrews achieved the "triumph of spirituality (*Geistigkeit*) over the senses; more precisely an instinctual renunciation" (1939a, p. 113).

The same triumph, however, brought the Hebrews closer to the memory of the "prehistoric tragedy," the murder of the primal father or fathers. Thus, while the Jews after Moses felt "superior to those who have remained in the bondage of the senses," they also felt burdened by a guilt that "clamored for recognition." Ambivalence, then, was inseparable from chosen-ness.

Once again, an episode in the history of psychoanalysis provided an uncanny repetition of an episode in Jewish history. The original Hebrews had chafed when they discovered that chosen-ness did not simply bestow a sense of superiority, but rather brought with it a gnawing sense of not living up to one's responsibilities. So, too, beginning around 1906, Freud was caught in the crossfire between two figures who sought a more affirmative psychology than Freud had provided. On the one hand, Carl Jung supported the idea of a psychoanalysis rooted in man's "higher"—that is, religious—self. On the other hand, Alfred Adler challenged Freud on behalf of the secular ideals of equal status and self-esteem. In retrospect one can see that Jung and Adler represented the two great movements that challenged psychoanalysis throughout its history: Christianity and socialism. These were also movements of enormous consequence for the Jews of Freud's time.

For Freud what was at stake both in ancient Judaism and in the conflicts that swirled around psychoanalysis was the subjectivity or inwardness of *Geistigkeit*, through which the mind rose above the clash of instincts and encompassed its own ambivalence. In his conflicts with Adler and Jung, Freud advanced this value by arguing that narcissism or chosen-ness was a bivalent or Janus-faced phenomenon that could not be approached in a one-sidedly affirmative way. In *Moses and Monotheism* he described the Christian and socialist faiths as shortcuts seeking to resolve ambivalence by bypassing guilt. For Christians, he wrote, the sacrifice of a son—"It had to be a Son, for the sin had been murder of the Father"—expiated the original murder. Paul, whom Freud called a Jew "with a gift for religion.... Dark traces of the past lay in his soul, ready to break through into the regions of consciousness," had intuited the truth of the primal murder, but only in the delusional form of "glad tidings." By contrast, the Jewish refusal of the "good news" of Christ's sacrifice was taken to contain an underlying message: "*We* did not kill the father, *you* did." Hence the Jews' rejection of salvation brought down an unending series of reproaches against them, as if they couldn't let the primal father remain buried, even after the crucifixion.

After the birth of Christianity, then, anti-Semitism changed its character. From a prejudice against a people perceived as alien, clannish, and stubborn, it became a prejudice against a people who reminded others of the fatal inevitability of guilt. When Freud met Jung, the eminently respectable son of a pastor, he hoped he saw a way beyond the anti-Semitism psychoanalysts faced. He "chose" Jung to become the "savior" of analysis, even urging his Jewish associates who did not like Jung to "cultivate a little masochism." Jung helped teach Freud the importance of the anthropology of early myth and ritual, and it was under the spell of his relationship with Jung that Freud wrote *Totem and Taboo*. The two men differed, however, in their interpretations of the unconscious. Jung, in the tradition of German idealism, believed that just as Kant had discovered the laws that governed conscious thought Freud had discovered the laws of the unconscious. Freud, by contrast, went back to *kedushah*—the law of the Father—in his discovery of the unconscious. His ultimate concern was with the individual soul and not with such anonymous, impersonal regulative principles as condensation, displacement, and considerations of representability, which Jung believed organized the collective unconscious of symbol and myth.

Sándor Ferenczi, one of Freud's closest associates, captured the difference between the two men. Jung's concern was the salvation of the community, not the analysis of the individual, Ferenczi wrote in 1912. Of course, it was Christ's sacrifice that laid the basis for the community's salvation. Thus Jung "identifies confession with psychoanalysis and evidently doesn't know that the confession of sins is the lesser task of therapy: the greater one is the demolition of the father imago"—the unconscious image of the father—"which is completely absent in confession." Jung sought to bring the patient to forgiveness and reconciliation, not self-knowledge; this in turn reflected on Jung. Jung doesn't want to be analyzed, Ferenczi wrote, but rather wants to remain to his patients "the *savior* who suns himself in his Godlike nature!" Being analyzed would entail exposing "his hidden homosexuality," that is, his identification with the band of brothers and refusal to recognize his ambivalence toward the father, Ferenczi continued. The band of brothers appears in Jung's writings as the "Christian community" or "brotherhood." Rather than make his own "homosexuality"—his "brotherly love"—clear to himself, Jung prefers to '"despise' sexuality" and praise "the 'progressive function of the [unconscious]'" (Brabant, Falzeder, & Giampieri-Deutsch, 1993, p. 417). A few months later, Ferenczi reiterated: "The *father* plays almost no role … the *Christian community of brothers* takes up all the more room" (Rieff, 1951, p. 121).

The conflict between Freud and Jung forced into the open the Jewish composition of psychoanalysis. The reason psychoanalysis had emerged among Jews, in Freud's view, was that the Jews were a people "especially sensitive to the repressed historical material that is their tradition," meaning, above all, guilt for the murder of the primal father (ibid.). Christians, by contrast, evaded the feeling of guilt, since Jesus' crucifixion redeemed the murder. Because, in Freud's thinking, self-knowledge necessitated an inner—personal—awareness of guilt and responsibility, it was harder for the Christian to engage in introspection than it was for the Jew. Thus, Freud explained to Karl Abraham, "Racial relationship brings you closer to my intellectual constitution, whereas [Jung], being a Christian and the son of a pastor, can only find his way ... against great inner resistances. His adherence is therefore all the more valuable" (H. C. Abraham & E. L. Freud, 1965, pp. 46–47).

In these and similar remarks Freud revealed himself to be a member of a parochial, still persecuted minority. For example, he seems to have known nothing of such great Christian thinkers as Augustine, Pascal, and Jonathan Edwards, whose critique of self-love or sense of the power of guilt are in every way the match of Freud's or the superior. Nonetheless, Freud's conceptualization of the unconscious as linked to the capacity to work with an analyst whom one could not see, touch, or feel also offered a riposte of sorts to Protestant philosophers like Hegel who called Judaism the religion of sublimity, meaning that Jews viewed God as all powerful and man as nothing. For Christians, the passion, suffering, crucifixion, and resurrection of Christ plunged the absolute into history and thus supplied the mediation through which humanity could touch and hear and feel God. Freud, by contrast, conceived of the analytic space as one in which patients could encounter what sometimes seemed to them a remote authority figure, someone whom they could not see and who offered no solace, no advice, no consolation, no relief from guilt. In working through a personal relationship to such a figure, Freud hoped that patients would reproduce infantile fantasies about the father and turn them into insight—what Ferenczi called "demolition of the paternal imago." Ironically, then, it was not the Jew but the Christian who, by substituting confession for analysis, left unanalyzed the transcendent, remote, sublime Godhead that Freud first called the primal father and later called the superego.

Adler's social-democratic and egalitarian critique of psychoanalysis complemented Jung's religiosity. Like the Hebrews who revolted against Moses, Adler sought an affirmative approach to narcissism. Thus, if Christians avoided the difficulties of self-knowledge by insisting that

Christ had already saved humanity, socialists held that the abolition of capitalism would produce universal benignity. Assuming that individuals had an
innate sense of dignity and self-respect, Adler (1909) explained "neuroses"
as arising from an insult or affront, such as the affront of poverty or dis-
crimination or what is known today as status injury. Sensitivity to slights,
he reasoned, was the real basis for class consciousness.[3] Any physician, he
continued, can observe this sensitivity in the transference. When the neurotic loves or needs, he or she feels "I am a slave." What Adler called the
"masculine protest" was the revolt against this feeling of enslavement in both
sexes. In 1911 Adler summarized his view: "There is no principle more generally valid for all human relationships than 'on top of' and 'underneath.'"

Freud called his "On Narcissism" (1914c) "the scientific settling of
accounts with Adler," meaning that he had situated narcissism within what
would soon be called the structural theory of the mind. In letters written at
the same time, Freud charged that Adler "tries to force the wonderful diver-
sity of psychology into the narrow bed of a single aggressive 'masculine'
ego-current," as if a child "had no other thought than to be 'on top' and play
the man." The view of life reflected in the Adlerian system, he added, "was
founded exclusively on the aggressive impulse; there is no room in it for
love" (1914d, p. 57). Adler and Jung complemented one another. For Adler
status was everything. Jung, by contrast, despised the ego's petty hurts, its
"oversensitivity," prickliness, its obsession with its standing in the world,
traits that he eventually associated with the Jewish character of psychoanalysis (Noll, 1994). Both men, however, sought to affirm narcissism without
recognizing ambivalence. Neither man accepted the difficult path toward
self-knowledge that Freud espoused in psychoanalysis, just as Moses had
espoused an equally difficult path in the form of monotheism.

There was a further analogue between Judaism and psychoanalysis,
especially significant for understanding America. Visiting New York, Jung
developed a theory (in terms we would now view as offensive) of the "Negro
complex," which paralleled Freud's theory of anti-Semitism. The Negro's
example, Jung believed, posed a threat to the "laboriously subjugated
instincts of the white races," just as the Hebrew rejection of Christ's sacrifice
reminded Christians of their guilt (McGuire & Manheim, 1994, p. 223). The
Negro, in other words, flaunted his or her sensuality, just as the Jews seemed
to Christians to flaunt the primal murder. Ferenczi elaborated on this idea
in a letter to Freud of July 9, 1910: "The persecution of blacks in America"
occurs because blacks

represent the "unconscious" of the Americans. Thus the hate, the reaction formation against one's own vices.... The free, "fresh" behavior of the Jew, his "shameless" flaunting of his interest in money, evokes hatred as a reaction formation in Christians, who are ethical not for logical reasons but out of repression. It is only since my analysis that I have understood the widespread Hungarian saying: "*I hate him like my sins.*" (ibid., p. 186)

The early conflicts in the history of psychoanalysis, then, parallel the early conflicts in the history of the Jews. Both pivot on the discovery that the "miraculous feeling," the "secret treasure," associated with chosen-ness was inseparable from an internal struggle over guilt and ambivalence. Jung sought to bypass that struggle by defining therapy in terms of the interpretation of a symbolic world that accompanied Kant's conception of reason. Adler, by contrast, anticipated the demand for recognition, which is the common sense of democratic societies today. Meanwhile, for Freud, the passage beyond the feeling of being chosen had to take place through recognition of the tragic weight of guilt, the subject of the next stage in Freud's schema (Rieff, 1951, p. 121).

Stage three: the fatal inevitability of guilt

In *Moses and Monotheism* Freud explained the inseparability of guilt from the Jewish love of God.

> Ambivalence is a part of the essence of the relation to the father: in the course of time the hostility could not fail to stir [again], which had once driven the sons into killing their admired and dreaded father. There was no place in the framework of the religion of Moses for a direct expression of the murderous hatred of the father. All that could come to light was a mighty reaction against it—a sense of guilt on account of that hostility, a bad conscience for having sinned against God and for not ceasing to sin. (1939a, p. 134)

Christianity, by sacrificing a son, had offered a one-sided—affirmative—solution to the problem of the Jewish bad conscience. The weakness of this solution revealed itself in the Christian inability to leave the Jews in peace. Instead, the church fathers adopted the Hebrew Bible as their own

"Old Testament," rewrote the Hebrew stories so that they foretold the coming of Jesus, insisted that the Jews be preserved as an example of error, and predicted that the second coming would be known by the conversion of the Jews. The radical character of *modern* anti-Semitism, culminating in Nazism, lay in its attempt to destroy the longstanding Christian dependence on Judaism, an aim symbolized by the Nazis' public burnings of the "Old Testament," a sacred text for Christians after all. For many Germans in particular the attempt to build a modern nation-state hinged on the effort to build a world without finance capitalism and without Bolshevism, in other words a "world without Jews" (Confino, 2013).

The weight that guilt plays in Jewish culture was also a problem for young Jews. Before the rise of the Nazis obscured everything else, emancipation implied freedom not just from Christian strictures but from Jewish strictures as well. World War I seemed a turning point. In 1917 the Balfour Declaration promised a Jewish homeland in Palestine. In the same year, the Russian Revolution ended the hated Romanov dynasty, originator of the modern pogrom and inventor of the greatest anti-Semitic lie of the modern world, *The Protocols of the Elders of Zion*. A great revolution swept the German-speaking Jewish world provoking complex rethinkings of Judaism such as those of Gershom Scholem, Martin Buber, and Franz Rosenzweig. Franz Kafka, who died in 1924, was increasingly read as a Jewish thinker as well as a Jewish writer. In the twenties, too, the correspondence between Freud and Einstein, encouraged by the League of Nations, symbolized the way the modern Jewish intellectual was becoming exemplary of Enlightenment values in general.

Freud's writings concerning the uniqueness of the Mosaic moment, the particular contribution of the Jews to world history, and the way in which modern scientific thought, including psychoanalysis, had transcended not just Judaism but all religion, were produced in this context, within which he saw Mosaic Judaism as providing a touchstone through which to interpret psychoanalysis. As the biblical text records, when Moses returned from Mount Sinai he discovered that Aaron had led the Hebrews in building a golden calf. "Make us gods, which shall go before us," meaning gods we can see, touch, and feel, the Hebrew people had cried out. That cry so betrayed Moses' messages that he ordered the sacrifice of three thousand Hebrew men and women who refused to follow him, all the while begging God to allow him, Moses, one look (Exodus 33–34). The insistence that one believe in a God that one cannot see and that thereby offered no sensual relief and consolation eventually led, according to Freud, to the murder of Moses. Just as the early Hebrews rejected monotheism, so in the 1920s two great alternatives to psychoanalysis beckoned: communism and America. Both appeared as salvation religions, offering powerful and appealing escapes from psychic conflict.

The charismatic and influential Wilhelm Reich represented the communist alternative. Terming matriarchy the familial system of "natural society," Reich praised "the natural self-regulation of sexuality that it entails" (1936, pp. 123–125). By contrast, the creation of patriarchy, private property, and the state constituted the Ur-repression from which all neuroses flowed. Working in "Red Vienna" with its working-class schools, libraries, community centers, and apartment blocks (one of them subsequently named for Freud), all aimed at creating *neue Menschen*, Reich urged the politicization of analysis. Attacking Red Vienna's "sexual abstinence" literature, he called for the sexual liberation of youth and women. The feminist psychoanalyst Karen Horney was among Reich's most devoted followers (Robinson, 1969).

The United States offered an alternative vision: individual rather than collective redemption. There the idea of mental healing, "mind cure," or "positive thinking," was close to a national religion, central to Christian Science, self-help ideologies, salesmanship, and career manuals, and movements for racial uplift, such as that of Father Divine. Mind cure preached "mind over matter," not in the sense of *Geistigkeit*, but in the sense of wishful thinking. In analysis the search for quick, affirmative shortcuts came from Sándor Ferenczi and Otto Rank, who suggested an "active therapy" in which the analyst prohibited activities such as masturbation or enjoined patients to fantasize, even suggesting the content of their fantasies (Ferenczi & Rickman, 1950, p. 193). Freud's goal of insight, Ferenczi and Rank explained (1925, p. 20), was "entirely different from the healing factor. … We see the process of sublimation, which in ordinary life requires years of education, take place before our eyes."

Freud was not immune to the appeal of either communism or emigration to the United States. On the one hand, he described himself as sympathetic to the "great experiment" unfolding in Russia while rejecting Reich's view that human beings are benign except insofar as they have been corrupted by property (Freud, 1927c, p. 8). On the other hand, he called the works of Rank and Ferenczi those of "children of their time … conceived under the stress of the contrast between the postwar misery of Europe and the 'prosperity' of America, and designed to adapt the tempo of analytic therapy to the haste of American life" (1937c, p. 215). In his late seventies and suffering from cancer since 1923, Freud responded to these challenges by deepening his stress on the role of guilt.

Freud didn't believe that patients came to analysts to get well; they came, rather, to satisfy powerful instinctual wishes that had been formed in infancy. For this reason, Freud insisted on "abstinence," meaning no consolation in the form of advice, sympathy, or recognition. In refusing to palliate the patient's situation, Freud's hope was that the instinctual need would be frustrated, intensified, and brought into sharper focus. Eventually, the need itself would become the object of observation and the result would be insight or self-awareness, in other words, *Geistigkeit*. However, the path to *Geistigkeit* was through the resistance: "No stronger impression arises from the resistances during the work of analysis than of there being a force which is defending itself by every possible means against recovery and which is absolutely resolved to hold on to illness and suffering" (ibid., p. 242). The key, then, was not to rest content with the *positive* transference, the desire for insight, but to also force the *negative* transference into consciousness. Only analysis did that (Freud, 1923b, pp. 12–59).

In the 1930s, two powerful forces converged to further focus Freud's imagination on the destructive drives: the difficulties analysts faced in gaining cures and the rise of new, radical forms of anti-Semitism, expressed in the German elections of 1930 in which the Nazis won the second-largest number of votes. After Adolf Hitler became chancellor on January 31, 1933, Germany began a series of careful, legalistic efforts to purge the Jews from cultural and economic life. In April 1933 the government ordered that no Jews could serve in an executive function in a medical organization. By 1934 more than half the Berlin Psychoanalytic Institute's former members had fled. Increasingly, the Nazi cataclysm threatened to swallow up the whole of Judaism, reducing psychoanalysis to a footnote in a larger tragic history. That was the context in which *Moses and Monotheism* was written.

One great idea pervades the book: the power of the command emanating from the law of the father and passed on unconsciously through evolution and history. In the course of its development, Freud wrote,

> A standard is created in the Ego which opposes the other faculties by observation, criticism and prohibition. We call this new standard the Superego. ... The superego is the successor and representative of the parents (and educators), who superintended the actions of the

individual in his first years of life.... The Ego is concerned, just as it was in childhood, to retain the love of its master, and it feels his appreciation as a relief and satisfaction, his reproaches as pricks of conscience. (1939a, p. 116)

Judaism, then, was a superego religion, an expression of the omnipotent, ubiquitous father. "What seems to us so grandiose about ethics, so mysterious and, in a mystical fashion, so self-evident, owes these characteristics to its connection with religion, its origins from the will of the father ... which sets out to work compulsively and which refuses any conscious motivation" (ibid., p. 122). For still obscure historical reasons, psychoanalysis had inherited both the burden and the opportunity of the Jewish relation to the father, as was shown in its focus on "abstinence" or sublimation. "While instinctual renunciation for external reasons is only painful, renunciation for internal reasons, in obedience to the demands of the superego [brings] a substitutive satisfaction. The Ego feels uplifted; it is proud of the renunciation as of a valuable achievement." Yet "the feeling of guilt is [also] created by the renunciation of aggression." "I consider this [idea] the most important progress in analysis," Freud added (Sterba, 1982, p. 116).

In February 1938 Adolf Hitler summoned the Austrian chancellor, Kurt von Schuschnigg, to Berchtesgaden, the resort town where *The Interpretation of Dreams* had largely been written. On March 11 the Germans marched without opposition across Austria's northern border and into Vienna, shattering Freud's fantasy that Hitler would be stopped at the city gates. Two days later, the board of the Vienna Psychoanalytic Society decided that all members should flee the country and establish the future headquarters of the society wherever Freud went. After disbanding the Vienna Psychoanalytic Society, Freud invoked the memory of Rabbi Jochanan Ben Zakkai who, after Titus's destruction of the second Jewish temple, fled to begin a school of Torah studies (Molnar, 1992, p. xxiv; Gilman, 1993, p. 35). He did not publish *Moses and Monotheism* until he migrated to England. With the destruction of analysis on the continent of Europe, and its rebirth in England and America, the fourth stage in Freud's schema unfolded: assimilation.

Stage four: assimilation and the matriarchal impulse

In *Moses and Monotheism* Freud used the transformation of Judaism into Christianity to illustrate the dilution and vulgarization that occurs when a difficult elite doctrine assumes a popular form. The new Christian religion, he wrote,

> meant a cultural regression as compared with the old, Jewish one, as regularly happens when a new mass of people break their way in or are given admission. The Christian religion did not maintain the high level in things of the mind to which Judaism had soared. It was no longer strictly monotheist, [and] it took over numerous symbolic rituals from surrounding peoples. (1939a, p. 88)

Unlike Judaism, too, Christianity "reestablished the great mother goddess and found room to introduce many of the divine figures of polytheism only lightly veiled" (ibid.).

Here, too, Freud's account of the fate of the Mosaic religion reflects his experience of psychoanalysis. The question of matriarchy or mother goddesses had arisen among analysts, along with the question of the role of the mother in psychic development, as a result of the rise of feminism, reflected in women's large and growing role within the analytic movement. Psychoanalysis was arguably the most woman-friendly profession in the world in the twenties and thirties, and Freud played a role in making this happen. For him, however, what psychoanalysis had in common with the Mosaic religion was not *patriarchy*, a word that came into use in the 1970s to signify female subordination, nor *misogyny*, a concept used in psychoanalysis in Freud's time but not at stake here, but rather the stress on *paternity*. Recognition of the father's role in procreation, Freud thought, had been a *cultural* advance, an aspect of the *Geistige* revolution that accompanied monotheism, insofar as the recognition of paternity had no clear instinctual or biological basis, as the mother–child relationship seemed to him to have. The idea of the Oedipus complex, the significance of sexual difference, and the exploration of the unconscious all presumed that prior moment of cultural advance. The stress on paternity did not deny the existence of a matriarchal or mother-centered phase in human history, but it did presume that the movement from matriarchy to what Freud called "the father-headed family" had meant the expansion of *Geistigkeit* in the sense of culture and law. In addition, for Freud, the analogous movement in childhood to the recognition of the father's role represented a developmental advance, one centered on the knowledge of sexual difference. The question, then, was not whether to integrate the matriarchal hypothesis into *Moses and Monotheism* but how.

Furthermore, Freud's discussion of matriarchy in *Moses and Monotheism* reflected the shift in psychoanalysis from the German-speaking world of central and Eastern Europe to Anglo-American liberalism and feminism. The first time that the issue of matriarchy surfaced in a major way in psychoanalysis was during Freud's conflict with Jung. Jung's emphasis on matriarchy derived from the romantic response to the Enlightenment and had a strong tie to the *Völkish* nationalism that eventually sanctioned the destruction of the Jews of Europe. Johan Jakob Bachofen's 1861 *Das Mütterrecht*, which linked mother-right to agriculture and the land, was especially important to Jung. Drawing upon Aryan solar myths as well as Bachofen, Jung in a letter to Freud of April 27, 1912 described the earliest societies as mother-centered and polytheistic. The mother "feeds" her favored *Völk*, while the role of the father is "purely fortuitous" (McGuire, 1974, p. 228). Behind incestuous wishes lies the desire to be a child again, in other words to be reborn. The purpose of analysis, Jung had urged in another letter to Freud of February 11, 1910, should be to "revivify among intellectuals a feeling for symbol and myth, ever so gently to transform Christ back into the [pre-monotheistic] soothsaying god of the vine, which he was" (ibid., pp. 18, 294; Jung, 1985).

By the 1930s, however, Freud was influenced by the mother-centered reinterpretation of psychoanalysis launched by Melanie Klein in London. In addition, he was struck by the excavations of Minoan–Mycenean civilization in Crete, which led to the remaking of our understanding of classical Greece, in part through James Frazer's twelve-volume compilation of fertility myths, *The Golden Bough* (1890), and in part through Jane Harrison's reinterpretations of Greek tragedy as portraying a conflict between chthonic mother goddesses and patriarchal militarized invaders. (Robert Graves was to continue this line of thought in *The White Goddess*, 1948.) After World War I Bronislaw Malinowski, a Polish emigré to England, returned from the Trobriand Islands claiming he could not locate a single myth of origin in which the father was assigned a role in procreation. This focus on the mother was social-democratic as opposed to *Völkish*. As many argued, social organization arose from the need for prolonged maternal care. For Lewis Mumford, for example, the maternal village was the forerunner of the paternal town (Stalley, 1972, pp. 289–380; Novak, 1995).

Like Jung, Freud believed there had been a transition from the "great mother" religions of tribes, in which men were only loosely attached to family life, to "father-headed" or pair-bonded families, but in Freud's view this was no loss. Rather, the transition accomplished an intellectual and spiritual gain. In his reasoning, while the father was not known in "primal hordes," one knew one's mother through direct sensory perception. Only after the murder of the primal father led to the creation of kinship relations, law, and the state—in short to the institutionalization of the oedipal order— did the cognitive, extra-sensual recognition of one's father become institutionalized. The creation of two-sex families in place of mother-centered tribes therefore signified the "victory of intellectuality [*Geistigkeit*] over sensuality [*Sinnlichkeit*]," in other words, the advance of reflective thought over sensory perception. In making this argument Freud was in line with much subsequent anthropology, such as the work of Meyer Fortes, who wrote, "Institutionalized fatherhood, unlike motherhood, comes into being not by virtue of a biological ... event, but by ultimately juridical, societal provision, that is by rule. Fatherhood is a creation of society" (Chapais, 2010, p. 196).

Freud's idea of a transition to "father-headed families" is enhanced by contemporary anthropological work reflecting the influence of Claude Lévi-Strauss. This work emphasizes the role of the "pair-bond" in creating the intense focus on kinship, which marked our species off. Recognizing the father's procreative contribution was critical to this break for two reasons. First, recognition of paternity made possible the sexual division of labor and thereby the prolongation of infancy, which led to the growth of the brain. Second, recognition of paternity made genealogy and kinship transparent and thereby useful for social organization, not loosely noted as they were when only the mother's role was apparent.[4]

The Hebrew Bible—Freud's subject in *Moses and Monotheism*—reflected an important moment in this evolutionary past. The shift from the mother-centered fertility goddesses of polytheistic Sumeria, Babylon, Canaan, and Egypt to Mosaic monotheism involved what David Bakan called paternalization, involving multiple changes at the levels of family life, genealogy, communal order, and political authority. As Bakan notes, it was probably the discovery of the role of the father that animated some of the excitement that went into the writing of the Bible. Bakan also notes that the Torah "is the product of a multitude of hands, and each hand that wrote was informed by many hands that spoke" (1979, pp. 13, 30). Furthermore, when Freud used such phrases as "the rule of the father," he generally had in mind not only the evolutionary past but also the Hebrew sense of a pervasive law or order having the family at its center. This was not the patriarchal family invented in ancient Rome and molded by the Christian focus on original sin, the condemnation of "concupiscence" (sexual desire) as an expression of love of self, and the exaltation of female virginity, but rather the patriarchal family of the Hebrew nomads.

Applied to Freud's own time, the conception of monotheism as an intellectual or spiritual advance was linked to the "dual-sphere" family, which was the family system in which Freud grew up. In Jewish history the dual spheres were the religious center (ultimately the synagogue) and the home; in Freud's day these had become work and the home. The underlying idea was of respect for the autonomy of each sex in his or her sphere. Properly speaking, the synagogue was not the Jewish form of such all-male institutions as men's lodges. Homosocial forms of that sort were premised on the derogation of family life, whereas the synagogue was the *complement* to home life. The dual-sphere family may have affected Freud's view that the sexes had the same early aims and objects and yet diverged essentially through the recognition of sexual difference. In any event, he equated this recognition of sexual complementarity and difference with *Geistigkeit* and placed it at the center of human development.

Moses and Monotheism also provided an evolutionary and historical counterpart to the discovery of the mother's role in psychoanalytic clinical practice. Just as Freud had turned the primal father into the superego, so he integrated the matriarchal archaeological discoveries into psychoanalysis. In 1931 he likened the psychic discovery of a pre-oedipal or matricentric stage of psychic development to the archaeological discovery of Minoan (i.e., pre-Mycenean) Greece. Everything, he wrote, "in the sphere of this first attachment to the mother seemed so difficult to grasp in analysis—so grey with age and shadowy ... that it was as if it had succumbed to an especially inexorable repression" (1931b, p. 226). During the pre-oedipal stage, Freud argued, psychic development was the same in both sexes. Later, however, during the oedipal stage, sexual difference became important, indeed, inescapable. At the same time, the early common path was critical to his reconceptualization of the oedipal stage. In the course of development, he wrote, "something which both sexes have in common [was] forced ... into different forms of expression" (1937c, p. 39). This common current Freud called the "repudiation of femininity," meaning the defensive repudiation of vulnerability in relation to the father. To be sure, the idea that the recognition of paternity represented a cultural advance could and did lead to sexist conclusions, such as the hypostatization of the mother's role in early childhood, which occurred in postwar United States and Britain. But these were not necessary, given Freud's emphasis on the psychic as opposed to the biologically given character of sexual difference.

Freud's conception of the psyche as marked off from the purely biological also found an echo in his approach to Jewish identity. According to the anthropologists and psychiatrists of Freud's time, the Jews were a tribe (*Stamm*) or a race (*Rasse*), which implied they were marked by a positive—in the sense of external or manifest—identity. It was thought, therefore, that the empirical sciences could identify the nature of the Jew through observation, measurement, or genetic tracking, a project on which the Nazis were already embarked when *Moses and Monotheism* was being written. Freud, by contrast, rejected the idea of direct, sensuous, concrete recognition of descent or racial identity. In effect, he was insisting that one could not know directly what it meant to be Jewish, just as one could not know directly who one's father was. Of course, this is true of all identity; there is always a cognitive or *Geistige* element that makes it impossible to know identity directly. In the late nineteenth century, however, this non-given element was posed as an accusation against the Jews. Richard Wagner, for example, reputedly called the Jews "the plastic demon of the decline of mankind," meaning, in other words, that they obscured the *Völkish* identity which Wagner sought to buttress (Ross, 2012; I have been unable to find the original source for this remark). Otto Weininger called the Jews "pervasively feminine," meaning that they lacked the autonomous Kantian ego that Weininger equated with masculinity (Sengoopta, 1996, p. 490). As these examples show, there was a connection between Jewish identity and gender identity, not because Jewish men were pervasively feminized, as some have argued, but rather because both Jews and women were questioning the derogation of their ascribed biologically given identities.[5]

There were also grounds for Freud's intuitions concerning the resonance between some forms of maternalism and the dilution or vulgarization of psychoanalysis. In England, Ian Suttie's 1935 *The Origins of Love and Hate* described Christianity as a "system of psychotherapy" in which matriarchal elements were central. Emphasizing the social over the individual, the external over the internal, and the altruistic over the selfish, Suttie called the Freudian emphasis on the father "a disease." In the United States, where a market society encouraged a narrow empiricism, and where the Calvinist heritage enfeebled explorations of the problem of guilt, the emphasis on the mother became linked to a de-emphasis of the unconscious. Gertrude Stein looked forward to an un-Freudian twenty-first century, "when everybody forgets to be a father or to have one." She broke with her brother Leo as a result of his decision to be analyzed, insisting that "If you write about yourself for anybody it sounds as if you are unhappy but generally speaking everybody ... has a fairly cheerful time in living" (Douglas, 1995, pp. 134–135, 139). These developments were underway when Freud wrote *Moses and Monotheism* as a contribution to what he hoped would be an eventual return of the repressed—the recovery of the original discoveries of psychoanalysis.

Soon after finishing the book, Freud died. With his death the question arises: will there be an analogue to the fifth stage in Freud's schema, in which the repressed tradition is rediscovered and reclaimed? Or would psychoanalysis become of merely historical interest? In *Moses and Monotheism* Freud wrote,

> It would be wrong to break off the chain of causation with Moses and to neglect what his successors, the Jewish prophets, achieved. Monotheism had not taken root in Egypt. The same failure might have happened in Israel. ... From the mass of the Jewish people, however, there arose again and again men who lent new color to the fading tradition, renewed the admonishments and demands of Moses and did not rest until the lost cause was once more regained ... It is proof of a special psychical fitness in the mass which became the Jewish people that it could bring forth so many persons who were ready to take upon themselves the burden of the Mosaic religion. (1939a, p. 176)

Is there an analogy to the prophetic tradition within psychoanalysis, for example in figures like Herbert Marcuse or Juliet Mitchell, who discovered radical trends in what others had taken as conservative, or in Jacques Lacan, who called for a "return to Freud"? Or has psychoanalysis already been decisively absorbed in a new eclectic mix of cybernetics, neuroscience, behaviorism, relational analysis, feminist therapy, and culture criticism, just as Judaism was absorbed into Christianity? Whatever we say about that, a prior question arises: How can we understand *Moses and Monotheism* so that it sheds light not only on the history of psychoanalysis but also on World War II?

Moses and Monotheism and the meaning of World War II

While writing *Moses and Monotheism*, Freud peered into the looming abyss of the Second World War almost as a dying person might look into an open grave. At the preconscious level he interwove strands from ancient Egypt, the Hebrews, personal memories, and the Jews of Europe with his own anxieties concerning the future of psychoanalysis. The result is a seminal text for understanding the war, comparable to works by exiles such as Erich Auerbach and Hannah Arendt and survivors like Primo Levi and Paul Celan. As I have argued, viewed as a meditation on the coming war, the book's central concern is the survival of *Geistigkeit* or spirit. Having endured the expulsion of the Jews from German and Austrian cultural and social life and the destruction of continental European psychoanalysis, Freud questioned whether self-knowledge would continue to be valued and whether the space in which self-reflective thought could unfold would be salvaged.

Simultaneously Freud saw himself as historicizing psychoanalysis, not only by seeking out its evolutionary and historical roots but also by situating it in the context of what was then called "Western" thought. He took the endangered state of psychoanalysis as a metaphor for the endangered state of Western civilization. In this sense the book effectively sought to define the values for which the war was about to be fought, even if Freud himself was only dimly aware of this. As we have seen, this gives the book its place in a family that includes Erich Auerbach's *Mimesis* (1946), Erwin Panofsky's "Renaissance and Renascences" (1944), Hans Baron's *Crisis of the Early Italian Renaissance* (1952), Karl Polanyi's *The Great Transformation* (1944), and Hannah Arendt's *The Origins of Totalitarianism* (1948). All these works pinpoint a transcendent value such as realism, single-point perspective, republicanism, or societal collectivity, identified with the ideals of subjectivity and democracy, which the war brought into crisis.

At the same time, *Moses and Monotheism* is a Jewish work: it belongs to the tradition of Jewish thought and is a product of the persecution of the Jews on the eve of World War II. Perhaps the best way to grasp this is by reference to Franz Kafka. Kafka was born, like Freud, in Moravia, one generation after Freud, and died another generation before Freud did. In both authors we have the vision of an all-powerful God or primal father, impossible to locate empirically, and an all-pervasive but fraying law (*Gesetz*), a patriarchal order, or even tradition, which cannot be directly accessed, whose claims are beyond rationality, and that leaves no place for the individual to hide. Kafka's writings represent the real-world external literary complement to the Freudian inner world, the unconscious turned inside out. Gregor Samsa actually wakes up as an insect, right in his own bed, an ego's defensive maneuvers dig out an underground burrow, the "instincts" take the form of speaking animals, bisexuality becomes a brother and a sister, and Joseph K. is not only irrationally guilty, he is also "shot like a dog." For both writers, the essential relationship is between "man" and God, or "man" and the Father, and is not the I-Thou relationship so favored in the Christian imaginary. Gershom Scholem captured the Jewish vision that the two authors share in a 1931 letter to Walter Benjamin that likened *The Trial* to the Book of Job: "Here for once a world is expressed in which redemption cannot be anticipated—go and explain this to the *goyim!*" (Horwitz, 1995, p. 23).

Freud's retelling of the biblical Moses story so that it centers on survival and transmission also belongs to such Jewish traditions as Talmud (commentary), *Zohar* (exegesis), and Haggadah (telling), especially because there is a strong paternal voice running through it. Auerbach's famous opening chapter in *Mimesis* describes the Hebrew mode of exposition as shaped by God's entry from some vast heights or depths, some "undetermined dark place," from which He or She calls: "Abraham!" So, too, did Moses enter Jewish life from some dark, undetermined place, leaving behind trails—archives for Jacques Derrida—of tradition, ritual, and law. Thus Freud argued that if a religious tradition were based only on conscious or explicit communication, "[I]t would be listened to, judged, and perhaps dismissed, like any other piece of information from outside; it would never attain the privilege of being liberated from the constraint of logical thought. It must have undergone the fate of being repressed, the condition of lingering in the unconscious, before it is able to display such powerful effects on its return, to bring the masses under its spell" (1939a, p. 101). Religious texts such as the Bible showed evidence of this long process of unconscious transmission and reworking. Thus Freud argued that Exodus—like all codifications of memory—had been "subjected to revisions which have falsified it ... mutilated and amplified it and have even changed it into its reverse" while simultaneously expressing a "solicitous piety [that] sought to preserve everything as it was" (1939a, p. 43).

Moses and Monotheism is also a work of Jewish testimony, written by a political refugee. While the Jews occupied a territorial kingdom for several centuries, they were *displaced*—in exile—when Moses found them and for most of the time afterward. That helps give the story of Moses its untoward power. The Hebrew people were not only the "founders" of Western culture—the originators of the idea of a single God, from which the whole of Christianity and Islam descend—but also "the Other" to the very culture they unwittingly founded. Their role as founders is crucial to understanding why anti-Semitism had the scope, power even—for its progenitors, as well as for its enemies, the majesty that it did, as we shall see. But the Jewish role as "Other" also anticipates the way the vortex of World War II's hurricane moved from Western Europe to the regions that Timothy Snyder (2010) has called "Bloodlands," such as Poland, the Ukraine, Byelorussia, and Western Russia, and then again to the struggles against colonization in Asia, Africa, and the Middle East and the postwar search for a new, extra-Western world order.

Exile, longing, and memory had been the locus of Jewish identity since the destruction of the Temple. The Hebrew liturgy states, "A fire kindles within me as I recall—when I left Egypt, but I mourn as I remember—when I left Jerusalem." The Haggadah enjoins, "In each and every generation let each person regard himself as though he had emerged from Egypt." Freud was himself an exile at both the beginning and end of his life. He made his childhood situation as an exile clear in an early dream discussed in *The Interpretation of Dreams* (1900). In the dream he saw himself almost in tears: "a female figure—an attendant or nun—brought two boys out and handed them over to their father, who was not myself." The dream, Freud wrote, concerned "the Jewish problem, concern about the future of one's children, to whom one cannot give a country of their own, concern about educating them in such a way that they can move freely across frontiers" (1900a, pp. 421–422, 426–428, 441–442). In associations to the dream, Freud recalled a Jewish asylum director who had been dismissed for confessional reasons, cousins able to flee Moravia for England during Freud's infancy, and a performance of Theodor Herzl's *The New Ghetto* (1894). He saw himself sitting at the side of a fountain in Rome weeping and recalled Psalm 137, the Israelite lament from the Babylonian captivity, "By the waters of Babylon we sat down and wept."

Because they were in exile, Ashkenazi Jews like Freud faced eastward. Just as in the anti-Semitic discourse of Freud's times, the Jews were "Asiatics," so many Jewish intellectuals believed that the spiritual center of Judaism lay in Poland, the Ukraine, and in the Russian Pale, as well as among the Sephardim and Mizrahim, rather than among the assimilated Jews of Germany and Austria-Hungary. Assimilated German Jewish homes were often filled with tallises, yarmulkes, tefillin, siddurim, and kashruth dishes from the East; Kafka's breakthrough writing came after he saw an East European Yiddish theater troupe perform in Prague. At the same time, the Jews poured into the modern universities, modern business, science, and literature. This posed a conflict in regard to Jewish identity. We can understand the conflict by contrasting Martin Buber's writings on the Hasidim, and his "I–Thou" philosophy, which originated during World War I, with Gershom Scholem's *Major Trends of Jewish Mysticism* (1941). Both Buber and Scholem believed that the renewal of Jewish life would come from the *Ostjuden*—from the East—but they had opposing views as to how this would happen. Buber used the Hasidic tales to stress the universality of the Jewish experience, especially its resonance with enlightened Christian themes such as the existentialist encounter. By contrast, Scholem drew on the Hasidim, and especially on their mystical currents, to emphasize Jewish difference, chosen-ness, and unassimilability. Freud was certainly closer to Scholem than to Buber on this divide, but he was even more radical in that he moved the *topos* of Jewish spirituality back in time and further East in space—to Egypt, the one Arab country of Freud's time that had a continuous history with the biblical era.

Egypt was a special passion for Freud. Although he had grown up in the shadow of the statue of Athena that stood in the Ringstrasse in Vienna, Freud was convinced that Athena was the descendant of the Egyptian phallic mother goddess Neith of Sais, the goddess of war. Isis, Osiris, and Horus were among his favorite antiquities, and when he visited London in 1908 he refused most invitations to tour, spending his evenings reading up for the next day's visit to the Egyptian rooms of the British Museum. When Freud first met Karl Abraham, he slipped two Egyptian figurines into Abraham's briefcase as a going-away present. When Abraham wrote on Ikhnaton five years later, Freud called the essay a new "orientation" for psychoanalysis, intending the pun. Like his contemporaries, Freud was especially struck by the discoveries of mother goddess figurines at the palace at Knossos (Crete), which many archaeologists believed was an Egyptian colony. In Freud's view, ancient Egypt was the most bisexual of all civilizations, and bisexuality for Freud laid the strongest basis for intellectual and artistic advance (Schorske, 1993).

The mystery of origins lies behind *kedushah*, which is as important as reason to *Geistigkeit*. Freud described Moses as a "Great Stranger." In fact, the Jews were "strangers" in Canaan before being enslaved in Egypt. When the Torah was written, the "Other" was Babylonia. The God of the Midrash was fashioned against the backdrop of the Byzantine Empire, and that of the Kabbalah against the backdrop of Muslim Spain. In *Freud and the Non-European* (2003) Edward Said wrote, "Freud was deeply gripped by what stands outside the limits of reason, convention and, of course, consciousness: his whole work in that sense is about the Other." According to Said, by locating Egypt *in* Israel rather than outside it, Freud was suggesting that there was something unknown, uncanny, and unconscious, at the center of Jewish identity (p. 54). There is truth in this—the truth of postcolonialism—but it is not the whole truth. Freud was not only putting Egypt at the center of Jewish history, he was also putting universality (*Geistigkeit*) at the center of all history, including that of the Jews. In that sense, *Moses and Monotheism* was exemplary of the Popular Front, the Marxist-inspired struggle against fascism. The Popular Front defined World War II as a conflict between those nations that descended from the Enlightenment, including the Soviet Union, and those that rejected the Enlightenment, led by Nazi Germany. For Freud, psychoanalysis was a child of the Enlightenment from which the concept of *Geistigkeit* derived.

Seen in that context, the attack on the Jews was not only an attack on the Jews as a people; it was also an attack on the civic republicanism of the Renaissance (Hans Baron, Erwin Panofsky), on the age of democratic revolutions (Karl Polanyi, Hannah Arendt), and on what Erich Auerbach called the tribal-democratic mode of representing everyday reality, which had begun with the ancient Hebrews. Freud, like almost all European analysts of the time, was a social democrat, not a classic free-market liberal, as he has so often been (mis)described, for example, by Peter Gay (2006). Still, it would be more precise to describe him as an important figure *for* the Popular Front than an advocate *of* it. In *Moses and Monotheism* he criticized the idea that consciousness can be traced back to so-called material factors and stressed instead the force of tradition, charisma, and "the personal influence upon world history of individual great men." Whatever the relation of Freudianism to the Popular Front, leftism had implications for Jewish identity. The Polish Jewish Trotskyist Isaac Deutscher grasped this in when in a 1958 lecture to the World Jewish Congress he described Freud as a "non-Jewish Jew." Praising "the Jewish heretic who transcends Jewry," Deutscher connected Freud to Heine, Marx, and Rosa Luxemburg, all figures who

were born and brought up on the borderlines of various epochs ...
where the most diverse cultural influences crossed and fertilized
each other. ... They were each in society and yet not in it, of it and yet
not of it. It was this that enabled them to rise in thought above their
societies, above their nations, above their times and generations, and
to strike out mentally into wide new horizons and far into the future.

In *Moses and Monotheism* Freud was trying to understand Jewish history, as
well as Jewish identity, but he was also trying to understand anti-Semitism,
not only in its ancient national and religious forms, but in its modern forms
as well. The Judeocide, to be sure, took place after Freud died, but the psychology that created and tolerated it was in place throughout the 1930s,
certainly in the German-speaking world. According to Mark Mazower
(1999), "National Socialism ... fits into the mainstream not only of German
but also of European history far more comfortably than most people like to
admit." Mazower had in mind especially Nazism's racial-nationalist welfare
system and its attempt to create a common European market, but Nazism
was also close to the European mainstream in its attempt to free European
Christianity from its dependence on the Jews. Richard Evans provides a clue
to the centrality of anti-Semitism to World War II in his review of Timothy
Snyder's *Bloodlands*. As Snyder argues, the Jews were killed along with Poles,
Ukrainians, Byelorussians, Roma, and many other peoples. Yet, according
to Evans, "There was something peculiarly sadistic in the Nazi's desire not
just to torture, maim and kill the Jews, but also to humiliate them. ... The
Slavs, in the end, were a regional obstacle to be removed; the Jews were a
'world enemy' to be ground into the dust" (2010, pp. 21–22).

Freud's book on Moses suggests how the idea of the Jews as "world enemy"
and the project of excluding them from the German nation and then extermi-
nating them could have gained such force. Judaism gave meaning to Nazism
in a way that the German struggle for continental hegemony, the *drang nach
Osten* (Eastern Europe and the Ukraine) in search of land, oil, and wheat,
or even the struggle for racial purity, did not and could not. Moses brought
the law to the Jewish people, especially the *Bilderverbot*; insofar as that step
concerned struggles with authority, tradition, and guilt, this step was philosophical as well as religious. From Freud's point of view, then, the covenant
between a single people and God began the long process of emancipating
humanity from the rule of the father. Nor were Jewish thinkers like Freud
alone in this view. For the Nazi revolution to be something more than a social

revolution or a ploy in Great Power politics—for it really to accomplish its revolutionary, thousand-year aims—it needed to accomplish a new founding of and for itself, one freed of the "unclean," "diseased," "foreign" element that had "contaminated" the German effort at transcendence until then.

Finally, then, we return to the question of Jewish survival. As a Jew of his time, Freud tried to clear away the brambles that underlay the refractory, conflict-ridden persistence of the Jews under conditions of exile, foreign occupation, persecution, and even genocide. In returning in a deeply personal, essentially autobiographical, way to the encounter between the Hebrew people and Moses, Freud was posing the enigma *of* the Jews as an enigma *for* the Jews. Writing when the question of Jewish survival itself was at stake, this reclaiming of the question of Jewish identity is among the book's enduring contributions.

Notes

1. This achievement, to be sure, was related to the problem of Jewish identity. For Freud, there was a *mystery* at the center of Judaism. In saying, as he often did, that he *did not know* what it means to be Jewish, Freud was also saying that not knowing was internal to Judaism.

2. In his Third Critique Kant wrote, "There is perhaps no passage in the Jewish law code more sublime than the commandment, 'Thou shalt make thyself no graven image nor any likeness neither of what is in heaven not beneath the earth.'"

3. Alfred Adler, "On the Psychology of Marxism," March 10, 1909, in *Minutes of the Vienna Psychoanalytic Society, vol. 2: 1908–1910*: 172–178. See also the minutes of June 2, 1909.

4. I should make clear that in situating psychoanalysis in relation to these three intertwined aspects of our species—the pair-bond, prolonged infancy, and kinship—I am not entering into current debates as to those aspects of evolution that are genetically transmitted and those that are properly cultural, but rather relying on what is sometimes called "deep history," history that includes our evolutionary past.

5. In recent years several thinkers such as Sander Gilman, Eric Santner, Jay Geller, and Daniel Boyarin have claimed to discover a link between women and Jews, generally along the lines of a supposed "femininity." No doubt there are many further complexities here.

References

Abraham, H. C., & Freud, E. L. (Eds.) (1965). *A Psychoanalytic Dialogue: The Letters of Sigmund Freud and Karl Abraham, 1907–1926.* New York: Basic Books.

Adler, A. (1978). Masculine protest and a critique of Freud. In: *Cooperation Between the Sexes* H. C. Anbacher, & R. R. Anbacher (Eds.). New York: Anchor.

Auden, W. H. (1940). In memory of Sigmund Freud. In: *Another Time.* New York: Random House.

Bakan, D. (1979). *And They Took Themselves Wives: The Emergence of Patriarchy in Western Civilization.* New York: Harper & Row.

Boyer, J. (1978). Freud, marriage, and late Viennese liberalism: a commentary from 1905. *Journal of Modern History, 50*: 91–99.

Brabant, E., Falzeder, E., & Giampieri-Deutsch, P. (Eds.) (1993). *The Correspondence of Sigmund Freud and Sándor Ferenczi, vol. 1: 1908–1914.* Cambridge, MA: Belknap Press.

Bultmann, R. (1956). *Primitive Christianity in Its Contemporary Setting.* Philadelphia, PA: Fortress, 1980.

Chapais, B. (2010). *Primeval Kinship: How Pair-Bonding Gave Birth to Human Society.* Cambridge, MA: Harvard University Press.

Confino, A. (2013). *A World Without Jews.* New Haven, CT: Yale University Press.

Douglas, A. (1995). *Terrible Honesty: Mongrel Manhattan in the 1920s.* New York: Farrar, Straus and Giroux.

Engels, F. (1884). *The Origin of the Family, Private Property and the State.* New York: Penguin, 2010.

Evans, R. J. (2010). "Who remembers the Poles?" Review of *Bloodlands: Europe Between Hitler and Stalin,* by Timothy Snyder. *London Review of Books, 32*(21): 21–22.

Ferenczi, S., & Rank, O. (1925). *The Development of Psychoanalysis.* New York: Nervous and Mental Disease Publishing.

Ferenczi, S., & Rickman, J. (1950). *Further Contributions to the Theory and Technique of Psycho-analysis.* London: Hogarth.

Freud, A. (1978). Inaugural lecture for the Sigmund Freud Chair at the Hebrew University, Jerusalem. *International Journal of Psychoanalysis, 59*: 145–148.

Freud, E. (Ed.) (1961). *Letters of Sigmund Freud 1873–1939.* London: Hogarth.

Freud, S. (1900a). *The Interpretation of Dreams. S. E., 4–5.* London: Hogarth.

Freud, S. (1910c). Leonardo da Vinci and a Memory of His Childhood. *S. E., 11*: 145. London: Hogarth.

Freud, S. (1912–13). *Totem and Taboo. S. E., 13.* London: Hogarth.

Freud, S. (1914d). On the history of the psycho-analytic movement. *S. E., 14*. London: Hogarth.

Freud, S. (1915e). The unconscious. *S. E., 14*. London: Hogarth.

Freud, S. (1923b). *The Ego and the Id. S. E., 19*. London: Hogarth.

Freud, S. (1927c). *The Future of an Illusion. S. E., 21*. London: Hogarth.

Freud, S. (1931b). Female sexuality. *S. E., 21*. London: Hogarth.

Freud, S. (1937c). Analysis terminable and interminable. *S. E., 23*. London: Hogarth.

Freud, S. (1939a). *Moses and Monotheism. S. E., 23*. London: Hogarth.

Freud, S. (1940a). An Outline of Psycho-analysis. *S. E., 23*. London: Hogarth.

Freud, S. (1976). *The Standard Edition of the Complete Psychological Works of Sigmund Freud*. J. Strachey (Ed. & Trans., in collaboration with A. Freud, assisted by A. Strachey & A. Tyson). New York: W. W. Norton.

Frosh, S. (2005). *Hate and the Jewish Science: Anti-Semitism, Nazism and Psychoanalysis*. Basingstoke, UK: Palgrave Macmillan.

Gay, P. (2006). *Freud: A Life for Our Time*. New York: W. W. Norton.

Gilman, S. L. (1993). *Freud, Race, and Gender*. Princeton, NJ: Princeton University Press.

Graves, R. (1948). *The White Goddess*. New York: Farrar, Straus and Giroux, 2013.

Hes, J. P. (1986). A note on an as yet unpublished letter by Sigmund Freud. *Jewish Social Studies, 48*: 322.

Horwitz, R. (1995). Kafka and the crisis in Jewish religious thought. *Modern Judaism, 15*(1): 23.

Jung, C. G. (1985). *Analytical Psychology: Notes of the Seminar Given in 1925 by C. G. Jung*. Princeton, NJ: Princeton University Press.

Kurzweil, E. (1989). Freud to Arnold Zweig, September 1934. In: *The Freudians: A Comparative Perspective*. New Haven, CT: Yale University Press.

Mazower, M. (1999). *Dark Continent*. New York: Alfred A. Knopf.

McGuire, W., & Manheim, R. (Eds.) (1994). *The Freud/Jung Letters: The Correspondence between Sigmund Freud and C. G. Jung*. Princeton, NJ: Princeton University Press.

Molnar, M. (1992). Introduction. In: *The Diary of Sigmund Freud, 1929–1939: A Record of the Final Decade*. New York: Charles Scribner's Sons.

Noll, R. (1994). *The Jung Cult*. Princeton, NJ: Princeton University Press.

Novak, F. G. Jr. (Ed.) (1995). *Lewis Mumford and Patrick Geddes: The Correspondence*. New York: Routledge.

Reich, W. (1932). *The Sexual Struggle of Youth*. London: Socialist Reproduction, 1972.

Reich, W. (1936). *The Sexual Revolution*. New York: Farrar, Straus and Giroux, 1963.

Rieff, P. (1951). The meaning of history and religion in Freud's thought, *Journal of Religion*, *31*(2): 121.

Robinson, P. A. (1969). *The Freudian Left: Wilhelm Reich, Geza Roheim, Herbert Marcuse*. New York: Harper & Row.

Ross, A. (September 25, 2012). The case for Wagner in Israel. *New Yorker*.

Said, E. (2003). *Freud and the Non-European*. London: Verso.

Schorske, C. E. (1981). *Fin-de-Siècle Vienna: Politics and Culture*. New York: Vintage.

Schorske, C. E. (1993). Freud's Egyptian dig. *New York Review of Books*, *40*(10): 35–40.

Sengoopta, C. (1996). The unknown Weininger: science, philosophy, and cultural politics in fin-de-siècle Vienna. *Central European History*, *29*(4): 490.

Snyder, T. (2010). *Bloodlands: Europe Between Hitler and Stalin*. New York: Basic Books.

Stalley, M. (1972). *Spokesman for Man and the Environment: A Selection*. P. Geddes (Ed.). New Brunswick, NJ: Rutgers University Press.

Sterba, R. (1982). *Reminiscences of a Viennese Psychoanalyst*. Detroit, MI: Wayne State University Press.

Zaretsky, E. (2006). The place of psychoanalysis in the history of the Jews. *Psychoanalysis and History*, *8*(2): 235–254.

Zaretsky, E. (2012). *Political Freud: A History*. New York: Columbia University Press.

CHAPTER TWO

Forgiveness in Judaism and psychoanalysis*

Stephen Frosh

Introduction

Freud's methodology as improved upon over the past hundred years allows us access to our minds in a unique and life-enhancing manner. It allows us to learn that what we take to be adult rational thinking is in fact infused with childhood imaginings, fears, hopes, and desires. This was recently brought to my attention in a dramatic Proust-like fashion when I began eating sweetened yogurt mixed with bananas. Suddenly I was back in my childhood kitchen surrounded, indeed enveloped, with the sensations, smell, and warmth of maternal love. I was retasting the sour cream, sugar, and bananas that my mother prepared for me. I was reexperiencing an idealized moment of my young life. This moment has been inside me all the time. The recent yogurt tasting and a host of other circumstances evoked the sensuality of that precious memory. It is of course not only sweetnesses from our past that remain inside us ready to emerge when we least expect it. We also contain an internal unconscious catalog of

*Parts of this chapter previously appeared in earlier versions in the following publications and are reprinted with permission: Frosh, S. (2012). The re-enactment of denial. In: A. Gulerce (Ed.), *Re(con)figuring Psychoanalysis: Critical Juxtapositions of the Philosophical, the Sociohistorical and the Political*. London: Palgrave. Frosh, S. (2013). *Hauntings: Psychoanalysis and Ghostly Transmissions*. London: Palgrave.

hurts, neglects, and frustrations that are also ready to emerge at times of their own choosing.

Those childhood pains when evoked by present-day circumstances are also linked to childhood versions of revenge. Which brings us to today's topic of forgiveness. Forgiveness, or not, like all such effectively alive experiences, is inexorably linked to our childhood ways of thinking and remembering. It's important to note that in spite of the richness of my bananas and sugar relived memory it is far from an accurate rendering of that early experience. My mother like all mothers was many things only one of which was sweet. Also sour cream is far from a health promoting snack for a young child and to tell you the truth I didn't even like it that much. My point is that the veridical truth of that moment is barely represented in this recovered memory. So too for the many hurts and neglects we have inside us. Alive in us, sure. Literally accurate, not so much. For some, the recovery of childhood hurts is an essential aspect of their psychoanalysis. Many have lived lives unknowingly twisted by the need to not remember. Often their bodies remember through multiple intractable pains. For others who don't seemingly recall, it falls on those intimates around them to suffer the slings from the original hurts. We find this to be a complicated and quite human story. Hurts that are often not recalled. Hurts that are recalled with vagary. Hurts that are often collected as a hobby that serve to hide other hurts. When we face the issue of hurts, which leads us to the issue of revenge, which leads us to the consideration of forgiveness, we are faced with a challenging task. What parts of today's bitterness relate to this adult moment and in what manner are they being colored by childhood perceptions and misperceptions. In a functioning psychoanalysis one of the tasks is to recall as vividly as possible and to relive in the moment with the analyst and thereby be able to reconsider from the perspective of adult wisdom. This goes for hurts, revenge, and, of course, forgiveness. And the forgiveness is not of the simple behavioral sort. Nor does it involve masochistic submission, turning the other cheek, or reaction formation. It is not anything that invalidates responsibility and it is something that can be both sought after as well as granted. This forgiveness is a capacity—a capacity to be free from an addiction to negativity, to be able to mentalize, to mourn. Ultimately, it is to discover the restorative love in one's own life; a love that needn't extend to the perpetrators of the hurt. The psychoanalyst Martin Bergmann offered his own summary of the subject: "Every attitude we have is a mixture of aggression and love including the relationship of our superego to our ego. If for whatever reason, prayer, or psychoanalytic work a shift has taken place in favor of love the subjective feeling of this shift will be experienced as forgiveness."

We have all read reviews about movies, often set in Manhattan, often of a small well-heeled group of individuals. The review says the characters were well drawn, the acting was nuanced, the plot moved along but there was something missing in the movie. There was something about the breadth of the human experience that wasn't represented in this movie.

Frankly I think the same could be said about my comments up to this point. To me they don't sufficiently reflect the breadth of the human experience. If we're going to take up the subject of forgiveness seriously we need to include in our considerations the full ugliness of the human experience. Unfortunately, in all of our lifetimes, we have seen more than our fair share of ugliness.

For example, in the 1940s the architects of the death camps celebrated their ability to murder hundreds of thousands of men, women, and children, innocents all, in as efficient a manner as they did. This is something different. Forgiveness?

We hear a lot of clichés about the subject of forgiveness. One that we all know is that "one should forgive but not forget." In our offices we often see situations where someone has forgotten but not forgiven. Some who have been through the camps have simply concluded, "forgiveness died at Auschwitz."

In 2001 there were large numbers of people who danced in the streets when they learned about the murder of the 3,000 innocents in the World Trade Center. They danced in the streets. This is something different. Forgiveness?

We are just like any profession in that we use jargon as shorthand to describe complicated states of mind. We have a concept, "the paranoid position." It represents a certain mindset in individuals and perhaps as well in cultures. Within this mindset all goodness is seen as belonging to oneself while all badness is seen as belonging to the other. As a result, empathy with the other's experience is neither valued nor desired. The capacity to mentalize, to use metaphor, is neither valued nor desired. The ability to mourn, to recognize ambivalence towards others, is neither valued nor desired. Alternatively, there is a mindset that is called "the depressive position." This mindset, which is characteristic of people who attend lectures on forgiveness, is characterized by an interest in the experience of the other. It values the ability to symbolize trauma and its affects. It recognizes the capacity to engage with and learn from reasonable amounts of guilt.

These differing mindsets impact how communities and individuals engage each other around aspects of forgiveness. If, for example, one attempts to discuss issues of injury and forgiveness and the participants do not recognize that those on the other side of the table are not working within the same set of meanings then it is unlikely to be an opportunity for shared understanding but rather more misunderstanding.

For example, in 2014 there were adults who handed out candy to children to teach them to celebrate the murder of other children. This is something different. Forgiveness?

We all know and have had the experience that to forgive is to the benefit of the forgiver. For me this raises the following question. If those who are in a position to be forgiven don't seek forgiveness, don't value forgiveness, and don't even know that they are in desperate need of forgiveness, does the consideration of forgiveness for them benefit the forgiver or coarsen the forgiver?

Harvey Schwartz

* * *

Miriam

In a well-known passage in the Book of Numbers or, to use its Hebrew name, "Bemidbar" (literally meaning "in the wilderness")—beautifully retitled by Avivah Zornberg (2015) as *Bewilderments*—Miriam is punished with leprosy for her leading part in speaking ill of her brother Moses' marriage to the Cushite Zipporah (Numbers XII). Aaron pleads with Moses to intervene, and Moses indeed prays to God, in five Hebrew words of great simplicity: "El na, refah na lah": "God, please, heal her." This is a deeply poignant moment. The hurt that Miriam has caused is set aside; the directness of Moses' appeal to God reveals its heartfelt nature: Forgive her, heal her; don't let the damage she has done prove irrevocable. God responds that Miriam must live outside the camp for seven days, and after that can reenter, enforcing a ritual of exclusion and reacceptance, of marking the sin and then letting it go. It is notable here that there is a tone more of sorrow over how Miriam has let herself down than of recrimination. The misdeed and the hurt that she has caused have to be acknowledged and cannot simply be ignored; nevertheless, there is a way back into the community.

Judaism is not always as forgiving as this, but in theory at least it promotes a philosophy and practice of reconciliation that is founded on acknowledgment of the reality of hurt, and of the importance of mechanisms of reparation. As the kabbalistic[1] myth of the shattering of the containers of divine light indicates (a myth to which I will return), the flaw in creation cannot be wished away: Damage will often be done, however carefully we might try to avoid it. There is a kind of "death drive" in operation, whether or not it is identical to the one Freud (1920g) invented; something that not only expresses *intentional* violence, but also simply trips us up when we think we have managed to stay level. But precisely because of this, Judaism recognizes that we need ritualizing remedies and that these must be allowed to set matters at rest. The sin-offerings, for example, described in minute detail in what for most of us are the dullest bits of the Torah,[2] testify to the importance of practices that will unbind the sinners from their sins, and bind them back *into* the community. Most strikingly of all, the possibility of being released from wrongdoing is emphasized in the ritual of the scapegoat, related in obsessive detail every Yom Kippur, the Jewish Day of Atonement, in which the high priest recants his own sins, those of his family, and those of the community—sins which are sent wandering out into the wilderness on the back of the luckless goat, so that it is the wrongdoings that are cast out, and not the doer of them. Notably, these examples have much to do with speech: Miriam's slander and the link between the ritual of the scapegoat and its replacement by the symbolic acts of Yom Kippur, when Jews list our wrongdoings individually and collectively, and ask each other for forgiveness. Maybe even the famous sequence of parashot[3] in Leviticus is relevant here: Acheri Mot, Kedoshim, Emor:[4] After death, holiness shall be spoken; or more familiarly, speak well of those who are not able to speak for themselves. Language, what is nowadays being called "injurious speech," is of central significance in hurtfulness and damage and also in remediating it. Zornberg (2015) notes the grammatically fanciful but homiletically convergent sources of *Midbar* ("wilderness") and *Davar* ("to speak"): It is through words that we are driven into the wilderness, and perhaps through words (the *Aseret Hadibrot*, the Hebrew term for the Ten Commandments) that we find our way out.

We already have a lot to think about here: What kind of actions demand forgiveness, and what kind can be forgiven? What is the place of ritual in this, and to what degree does it depend on an inner sorrowing and acknowledgment of having done wrong; most of all, perhaps, are there conditions under which forgiveness makes no sense at all, in which the wrongdoer can never expunge the destructive act? And given the claim that psychoanalysis is immersed in Jewish thought, can psychoanalysis be viewed as a modern ritualizing remedy? If so, who or what is being held responsible for the damage we do to ourselves and others, and who should be forgiven?

One thing to note about the biblical episode with which I began is that it is the victim—Moses—who appeals for forgiveness for the "perpetrator," if we can use that term, Miriam. His love for her, this sister who watched over him in his earliest period of life and in whose merit the Israelites have been kept watered throughout their travels in the desert,[5] triumphs over any feelings he might have of being betrayed. "El na, refah na lah." In addition, something not accidental to my own interests and arguments, the hurt is over a moment of racism and repudiation of difference: Moses had married a Cushite, perhaps an Ethiopian, a black woman. Rashi[6] suggests that there is a link between the terms "Cushite" and "woman of beauty," both Hebrew words having the same numerical value; however one reads this (Rashi says about Moses' wife, "Everyone agreed she was beautiful just as everyone agrees a Cushite is black"), it suggests the operation of envy as the source of slander. Something pernicious and modern operates here, with which we are all too familiar: the denigration, in words and deeds, of racialized others. If there is a lesson here it is that if we are truly to be able to seek forgiveness and reconciliation wherever there is conflict, we need to acknowledge how racism and disparagement of others can even creep into "Jewish" sensibilities. Moses, the greatest prophet in Judaism, "whom the Lord knew face to face," married a black woman; and his family was punished by God when they complained.

But let us get back to the main point. What counts here is that forgiveness comes from Moses and then from God; the one who has been wronged is the only one who can decide to forgive and who can ask for the punishment meted out to the wrongdoer to be ameliorated. There is a Jewish principle at work here: At least in cases of human-to-human wrongdoing, one has to forgive a perpetrator who asks genuinely for forgiveness; this genuineness includes full acknowledgment of what was done. But what can this mean, psychoanalytically speaking, and what is it we can forgive?

An uncomfortable history

My own perspective on psychoanalysis is not primarily a clinical one though I have great respect for, and some experience of, its clinical practice.

I have no doubt that at the level of this practice, it might be possible for a patient who has been hurt, or feels her- or himself to have been hurt, to find ways to be released from that hurt, which may or may not involve forgiveness. I tend to think of one part of the process of psychoanalysis as a kind of "unbinding" (which itself has biblical resonance); in this instance, if we are bound to those who have injured us, and to those who we have injured, through a situation of continuing irresolution, then perhaps one thing psychoanalysis might offer is a route to some freedom from this binding through seeking or giving forgiveness. It might also be relevant to consider the moments in which the *analyst* seeks a kind of forgiveness from the patient. The American psychoanalyst Jessica Benjamin has theorized this in detail with her notion of the "moral third," which she defines as "the courage for the nonjudgmental awareness that honestly recognizes moments of dissociation, misattunement, defensiveness—aspects of what was called in the narrow sense countertransference" (2009, p. 442). That is to say, analysts might have to take responsibility for their missteps and not interpret everything as a reflection of the patient's unconscious state of mind. This clinical notion is also used by Benjamin to think about issues of responsibility in the political field, somewhere "outside the clinic." Put simply, the analyst will not have caused the patient's original injury, but however skilled she or he is, there will be moments of *injuriousness* in which, as Benjamin puts it, the analyst "bumps into the patient's bruise." The clinical responsibility to note and acknowledge this becomes a political–ethical responsibility to respond to the bruising of the other that a witness (i.e., one who has not initiated the original injury) participates in through associating with oppression, or through failing to take up an active stance against it. This happens in every time and place in which we are called upon to take a stand—to become the moral third—yet are tempted to shy away from this call.

Thinking about psychoanalysis as an institutional and political practice, however, there are a number of complexities to deal with. I see psychoanalysis as a critical discipline in its essence, by which I mean that it raises a lens to individuals and to society that challenges them to think honestly. In the name of a kind of truth, however slippery that concept might be, it demands that people do not deceive themselves; and it refuses to take at face value the claims that are made about them. Despite this, psychoanalysis has not always found it easy to face up to its own historical truths. I want to spend a short while on this, focusing on one episode of clear relevance to the issue of Jewishness and psychoanalysis, not as an attack on psychoanalysis but rather as an object lesson in how hard it is to get to that stage of asking forgiveness that I mentioned before. In order to be an ethical practice, which is how I see psychoanalysis, there is often some darkness that has to be faced—and psychoanalysis as an *institution* has not always been so good at holding up a torch (which is not a statement about individual psychoanalysts, many of whom have been very brave in sometimes dangerous circumstances). My example here comes from something I worked on in my book *Hate and the Jewish Science* (Frosh, 2005): the attempt by the International Psychoanalytical Association (IPA) to find a way of dealing with the legacy of the actions of the German psychoanalysts in the period of the Third Reich. One focal moment for this was at the IPA Congress in Hamburg in 1985, which I shall briefly describe; another was in the Berlin Congress of 2007, which I have written about subsequently (Frosh, 2012) and will return to equally briefly in a moment.

There are now many places in which the history of German psychoanalysis' engagement with Nazism is dealt with in detail. This work has shown clearly that the psychoanalysts followed a policy of "appeasement" towards the Nazis, characterized by an attempt to distance psychoanalysis from its "Jewish" elements; that this resulted very quickly in the cleansing from the German Psychoanalytic Society of its Jewish members; and that the non-Jewish analysts who thereafter constituted the Society maintained their activities throughout the period of the Third Reich, mostly in congruence with the regime. For many years, this history was largely hidden, as the psychoanalysts set about rebuilding their organization and their myths, presenting themselves—like many other Germans—as always having been victims and possibly opponents of Nazism (Brecht, 1995). It was only at the first postwar congress to take place in Germany, the Hamburg Congress of 1985, that the real history broke into consciousness. More than anything else, this was through an accompanying exhibition, recorded in Brecht, Friedrich, Hermanns, Kaminer, and Juelich (1985), which revealed to the psychoanalysts in an "undeniable" way, through documents and photographs as well as an understated commentary, simply how far the collaboration with the Nazis had gone, and how impossible it would be to see this as anything other than a betrayal of the Jewish analysts, and of psychoanalysis itself. It is this heritage with which the "returnees" to Germany for the two congresses had to contend.

Not everything that goes on in conferences relates closely to the main event; people have their personal and professional agendas and interests, and many of the papers that are given there could be given anywhere in the world. This was no less true of the Hamburg and Berlin IPA Congresses than of any other, but it is nevertheless the case that everything that happened in both places seems to have happened under the shadow of the "return to Germany," and could not escape the issue of what it means to have a Nazi past. In this regard, the Hamburg Congress got off to a good start. The congress was opened by the mayor of Hamburg, Klaus von Dohnanyi, who gave a remarkably well-informed and direct presentation of the issues and feelings that were involved in holding the congress on German soil. Von Dohnanyi noted that the exhibition had revealed the equivalence between the actions of psychoanalysts during the Third Reich and those of other Germans, even those who might seem well intentioned. "For fear of losing everything," he said, "bit by bit was sacrificed, every step being rational—and yet at the same time always in the wrong direction. Here a compromise concerning persons, there a compromise of principles, but always in the pretended interest of preserving the whole—which in the end was lost" (Opening Ceremony, 34th IPA Congress, 1986, p. 4). Von Dohnanyi then asked whether psychoanalysis could "help us not only to understand ourselves better, but also to be and act better"; his doubts on this subject were clear for all to see. And finally, looking the issue of acknowledging the past through identification straight in the face: "Whoever says: our Bach and our Beethoven, must also say: our Hitler. This, too, will be one of your topics" (ibid.).

Actually, it was not. Instead, one could see at work in the congress clear instances of what psychoanalysis itself recognizes as *denial*. There was praise for the achievements of the German Psychoanalytic Association (which was formed in 1950 as a way of regaining acceptance by the IPA, but which itself contained collaborators) in recuperating German psychoanalysis after the war, and there was an account of psychoanalysis as one of the *victims* of Nazism, but there was little that examined the German psychoanalysts' culpability. There were references later to the power of the emotional atmosphere of the congress and claims that the effect of this was that by its end "Our German colleagues were not only colleagues but very often friends" (Weinshel, 1986, p. 89), as if reconciliation and forgiveness had been wrought. However, it is clear from the accounts of others present that not everyone agreed. Rafael Moses and Rena Hrushovski-Moses (1986) spoke on behalf of many Jewish analysts when they expressed their unease and disappointment. "We left Hamburg before the official farewell party," they wrote (p. 175). "We were feeling vaguely depressed. The general atmosphere was that something had been missed. The central issue of this Congress—that it was the first one to be held in Germany since the Second World War and since the Holocaust—had been very much in the air but had not been adequately dealt with."

They go on to describe a sequence of events during the congress in which both German and non-German (including Jewish) analysts stepped back from confronting the feelings swirling below the surface, as if they did not want to risk blowing something fragile apart. In what might perhaps be seen as a common defensive move, the past was invoked precisely in order that it should *not* be fully faced—that is, sometimes a way of not dealing with something is to talk about it as if it has already been resolved. "We should move on," can be a powerful defensive move. Moses and Hrushovski-Moses suggest that behind all this there was a complex of dynamics, including particularly a fear on the part of German analysts that they were going to be attacked, so that they and the organizers of the congress worked hard to avoid confrontations; and a complementary sense among non-German analysts that they wanted to move on, "that the Germans of today could not and should not be held responsible for what their parent generation had done; that peace must be made and the past put aside" (p. 179). The concern then became that the congress should "go well" rather than deal with the issues, the kind of thing that often happens—in the service of denial—both in individual psychoanalytic sessions and in organizations and meetings of all kinds. In a paper on the Hamburg Congress, John Kafka (1988, p. 299) writes, "I have seen in myself, in German and non-German colleagues, and despite the most serious efforts to 'deal' with the Holocaust, an impatience, a wish to move away from the topic." There may also be something else at work, connected to finding oneself in what still amounts to an anti-Semitic society, or at least a society in which anti-Semitism has not been eradicated.

It should be clear that no one is being accused of bad faith here: As is commonly the case, everyone seems to have worked toward the success of the congress both in terms of its smooth running and as an attempt to manage something of an encounter with the Nazi past. The meaning of meeting on German soil was certainly not ignored. Yet, it is equally clear that the overall feeling was of something missed, a chance not taken, a coming-together that looked like an "event" but was actually a ritual, which made it possible to claim that an important thing had happened as a way of contributing to a defensive process. The parallel is perhaps with the ambivalent patient (which may mean, *every* patient) who turns up to psychoanalysis precisely in order to stay the same; that is, the mere act of turning up is mistaken for doing the work, or is even an excuse for not doing it ("I am going to analysis, so that's enough; I don't need to take any further responsibility"). The psychoanalytic community certainly turned up in Hamburg, and it was clearly challenged by the exhibition, by the mayor, by the exposure of Germans and Jews to one another, by the reminders in the external situation. Yet little was grasped hold of, with the consequence that no resolution could be achieved, but the cancerous mistrust and disturbance of unacknowledged yet deeply felt emotions continued to fester. This is all to say that "identification," which was the official theme of the Hamburg Congress, was indeed a very present issue, but it was managed in a way that dodged the central question, nominated afterwards by the analyst Janine Chasseguet-Smirgel (1987, p. 437) as, "*What is one to do with a Nazi father?*"

In the light of this, it is perhaps no surprise to hear that the next attempt to face up to this history on German soil, in the 2007 Berlin Congress, also had its very difficult aspect, despite the passage of time. I won't labor the point here, but it is nevertheless instructive to notice that the organizers of the congress set up a kind of "container" for the tension involved in the "return" to Berlin, and then systematically—if unconsciously—undermined it. I am referring here to a group called "Being in Berlin" that was set up for anyone to go to who wanted to do so, explicitly as "an opportunity for all who may wish to pause to reflect on their experience and to express personal thoughts and feelings" (Erlich, Erlich-Ginor, & Beland, 2009, p. 811). The agenda was thus clearly stated: to offer a space for reflecting about "personal thoughts and feelings" generated by the experience of being in Berlin. What happened, however, was not only that such reflection occurred, as one would expect, but also—and perhaps one would expect this too—that the institutional setting, the congress itself, enacted something around the group that revealed its own powerful "unconscious." That is, the setting both encouraged the articulation of feeling and at the same time, in a classic enactment of ambivalence, blocked its resolution. This all happened around the administrative arrangements for the group, which in a profession that takes very seriously the conditions under which it practices (the regularity of time and space, in particular) is exactly where one might look for symptomatic behavior. That is, because psychoanalysis gives priority to the safety of the "setting" as a way of "containing" the flow of unconscious processes, these processes push precisely at the seams of the setting in order to make themselves felt.

The key symptom of this kind was the difficulty the organizers had in timetabling the group appropriately, as if it always slipped out of mind. "Although the event had been discussed and formulated long in advance," the organizers note (ibid., 2009, p. 813), "it turned out that, while the time slot was indeed the same every day (something we insisted on), the same space could not be; we would have to 'wander' or 'relocate' ourselves to a different room each day." These words, "wander" and "relocate" are clearly not neutral, but are chosen to resonate with the impact of Nazism itself, and with its effects on psychoanalysis: "It is a new kind of diaspora," as Anna Freud famously commented in the 1930s (Steiner, 2000). But even this enforced nomadism did not fully encompass the degree of institutional acting-out that the Being in Berlin group produced, even before it had properly got going. Not being sure how many people would attend, the group conveners had accepted a relatively small room for the group. About twenty-five chairs were laid out, lecture style, facing the front despite the organizers' request for a circle; and when people started to arrive it rapidly became clear that the room would not be able to hold them all. What happened next—and one has to recall that these are psychoanalysts that one is reading about—is eerie in its recapitulative power.

> The behaviour was both frightening and troubling: while 60 or 70 people were quite uncomfortably squeezed into the room, there seemed to be twice as many outside the door trying to get in. A struggle developed between the people standing inside and those outside. There were feeble attempts by those standing in the doorway to explain that there was no more room, and the noise from the hall was quite disruptive to whatever was beginning to transpire inside. Finally, there was a decisive slamming shut of the door. Immediately, associations came up from the group of being "squeezed into a cattle car" and the "doors being shut as in the gas chambers." (ibid., p. 814)

For the second day, the congress organizers arranged a larger space. However, rather than the "container" referred to in the announcement of the group event, this turned out to be "a non-existing, 'fabricated' room" (ibid.), a foyer space from which a number of doors led to other panels taking place at the same time—doors which "had to be closed and guarded by specially hired personnel" to make sure there were no interruptions. Apparently for safety reasons, only fifty chairs were initially supplied. More chairs had to be gathered, people grabbed them "sometimes violently" and someone was hurt, and "The rapid, rhythmic metallic sound of chairs being dislodged from the carriers was constantly in the background and several people associated it to the sound of trains" (p. 814).

It is one thing to recognize the impact of these disruptions on the frame of analysis, and another to be sure of their source. Erlich et al. are in no doubt about the former, and seem to see the pain involved as having been in some ways conducive to their task.

> Attempting to provide a space for feelings and associations evoked images in the participants of the slamming shut of boxcar doors and the sound and sensation of trains; angry wishes for the "conductor"— the leader or Führer—to act more forcefully in order to establish order in the chaotic situation; aggressive shouts and objections directed at the congress photographer who tried to take pictures, and so on. These were readily available associations and recapitulations. They testify to the poignancy and aliveness of the associations, symbolizations and feelings about Nazi Germany and its atrocities. (pp. 814–815)

This all rings true, but to my mind there is something else going on here as well. How could it be that the sophisticated psychoanalysts who set this up could not predict that there would be this powerful enactment, as well as the resurfacing of what the organizers are not afraid to name as anti-Semitism in some of the contributions to the group itself? My own view is that there remains something lacking in the psychoanalytic heritage, which is a genuine coming-to-terms with the Jewish part of that heritage—a very large part, as we know—and with the immense injury done to it by the custodians of that heritage themselves. Can the present-day leaders really face up to it so that some kind of resolution in forgiveness can be managed; or are we likely to see repeated *enactments* in place of a genuine working through? Something poisonous seems still be alive, and psychoanalysis itself is not free of this.

On shattering the vessels

My excursus through a painful element in the history of psychoanalysis, was, I want to repeat, not intended as an attack on the discipline, but as a lesson in starting at home before preaching to others. Again using Jessica Benjamin's "moral third" framework, we need to find ways of acknowledging what happens even in what might appear to be the most enlightened insti-tutional settings. What can be more astute than psychoanalysis, a reflexive practice that examines carefully and rigorously every element of its own behavior for signs of unconscious blocks and destructive impulses? Yet even in those circumstances, things go wrong. And we might ask whether there is something in the encounter with Jews and Jewishness that is both exciting and toxic, making the ground especially slippery, and not just for psychoanalysis.

I want to move onto slightly safer, if more esoteric, ground now. Is there something that psychoanalysis can derive from the Jewish encounter with forgiveness? That might sound an odd way around—why not ask instead what Jews can gain from psychoanalysis' teachings on how to forgive? But I am taking seriously here the idea that psychoanalysis draws on some Jewish perspectives, and want to reintroduce what some of these might be in our particular area of interest. Paramount here is a line of thought around what it might mean to recognize the reality of human destructive-ness and to try to find ways of facing up to it that lead not to recrimina-tion but to reparation. An example is the claim (Lutzky, 1989, p. 449) that there is "a striking congruence between the Kabbalistic myth of *tikkun* and the Kleinian concept of reparation, both metaphors of creation, frag-mentation, and re-creation—of the mystical cosmos on the one hand, of the internal object world on the other." These two powerful ideas do indeed have many parallels, particularly in the way they operate as individual and communal responses to human destructiveness. *Reparation* refers to "the variety of processes by which the ego feels it undoes harm done in phan-tasy, restores, preserves and revives objects" (Klein, 1955, p. 133). *Tikkun* is the Kabbalistic term for complex processes whereby the shattered "vessels" that contained the divine light of creation are made whole by the acts of humans—particularly Jews, whose task this is—who repair the broken shards and recover aspects of the Divine from the shadowland into which it has fallen. Both these sets of images are responding to a very widely felt psychological sensation of guilt arising from a consciousness of destructive-ness; both of them also have historical resonance, in Klein to the devastating impact of the world wars of the twentieth century and in Lurianic mysticism to the historical disaster of the expulsion of the Jews from Spain at the end of the fifteenth century. "How could such events come about?" each theory might be understood to ask. Because we are challenged, seems to be the answer—in the one case to find sources within ourselves to enable us to overcome and make good our destructiveness; in the other to formulate a way forward in relation to finding the Divine light even in what seems to be utter darkness, and repairing it.

It seems likely that such parallels between some core psychoanalytic concepts and those to be found in the Jewish mystical tradition have some validity, but perhaps this is mostly because such concepts gain their potency and durability because they refer to widely shared dilemmas—in this case, how to deal with guilt, loss, and the sense of unreasonable punishment. Whether this is a specific and meaningful link between psychoanalysis and Judaism is another matter: It is very probable that similar parallels can be found with many other traditions, as studies of Christianity, Buddhism, and so on all testify. Nevertheless, Jewish mysticism has its own profound dynamic, especially grappling with issues of exile and *"hester panim,"* God apparently wantonly turning His face away from those who need Him. This suggests at least one route of connection between psychoanalysis, with its Jewish heritage, and Judaism, or Jewish experience. It has sometimes been suggested that psychological suffering is a kind of exilic state, a separation from one's self. I am not overly keen on this idea, as it implies that against such an "exile" there is a true state of identity that represents well-being and integrity, a kind of wholeness or "home" to which we might all aim to return. I see this as a kind of regressive fantasy which is contradicted by the psychoanalytic revelation of how each of us, as a human subject, is "split," and how our identities are multiple, fragmented, and conflictual. We are never fully at home with ourselves; this is a *psychoanalytic* notion, expressed in Freud's (1916–17, p. 285) famous remark that psychoanalysis is a blow to narcissism, because it demonstrates that the ego is not even "master in its own house." There is even a biblical link with this idea. When the patriarch Jacob thinks to settle down in his old age, the text seems to be about to recount his achievements, but gets nowhere. All it says is, "These are the progeny of Jacob. Joseph, being seventeen years old, was feeding the flock with his brothers ..." (Genesis 37, 1–2). Rashi's commentary is the building block here:

> Jacob wanted to live at ease, but this trouble in connection with Joseph suddenly came upon him. When the righteous wish to live at ease, the Holy One, blessed be He, says of them, "Are not the righteous satisfied with what is stored up for them in the world to come that they wish to live at ease in this world too?"

What can be seen at work in this passage is a strikingly psychoanalytic idea: that we become "settled" only at the price of relinquishing our awareness of our deeply "unsettled" nature, the way a certain kind of "trouble" or disturbance is a condition of our being. We wander all the time, seeking somewhere to take rest but knowing that this is not fully achievable: diasporic consciousness, in this regard, is not an accident, but something intrinsic both to Jewish life and to psychoanalysis. Under such circumstances, we never reach a restful state in which destructiveness is completely averted; reparation, *tikkun*, and forgiveness are endlessly necessary.

It is perhaps in this context that it is worth returning to the idea of reparation as a mode of forgiveness. This is a difficult set of arguments, so I will try to be clear at the risk of simplifying rather too much. In the Jewish mystical tradition, as described in an unsurpassed way by Gershom Scholem (1941), the kabbalistic imagery of the breaking of the ten *sefirot*[7] during creation is a cataclysm: They were meant to hold the divine light and their loss scatters this light everywhere, producing an exile of the divine that forces history into motion as a process of suffering and searching until the scattered sparks can be redeemed. What this suggests is that at some point in time—usually referred to as the coming of the Messiah—there will be a gathering in of the exiles and a new era that is radically distinct from all that has gone before. At its simplest, the rent universe will be repaired, made whole again. I see this as a metaphor of forgiveness: the damage that we perpetrate is made good by the way in which we perform *mitzvot*,[8] acts of reparation. But it is also possible to read the sparks differently, not as a kind of failure, but rather as a way of indicating that there are various forms of holiness in the world that need to be treasured for their own being; that is, we should find ways to acknowledge things that have been lost or abandoned, and value them precisely in their exilic, diasporic state. This is why the contemporary social philosopher Judith Butler (2012) emphasizes the idea put forward by Walter Benjamin that the "flashing up" of the lights of the *sefirot* should be understood to express the possibility that those who have lost most and who are written out of humanity have the chance to return, to make their presence felt. This suggests that a precursor to forgiveness is *justice*, and even before that comes the requirement to *remember*, to ensure that what has been hidden from consciousness is not completely lost.

Social forgiveness

In his "Theses on the Philosophy of History," Walter Benjamin (1940) asserts the necessity of recognition of the past in the present; without such recognition, the past disappears. "For every image of the past which is not recognized by the present as one of its own concerns threatens to disappear irretrievably," he writes (p. 247). The incitement to remembrance that Benjamin references directs us to continually re-examine the past, to keep it in the present as a living entity, not only as a memorial to something lost. What happened, what was done, what is the legacy? Especially, what injustice does it speak of that penetrates the present in barely visible streams of dust and smoke? The dust of historical oppression; the smoke and fumes of past destruction; these vapors drift across time and are breathed in by every generation—ghostly emanations that infiltrate the present, structuring it and giving it meaning, and sometimes poisoning it too. And the future? The future is only sustainable in the present as an openness; but this might mean that something has to be forsaken, or forgiven, something has to be let go of or overcome, before we can learn to move on.

I am suggesting here that memory and forgiveness have to run together, and that this is part of the relationship between a kind of Jewish sensibility and the question of what sorts of conditions can give rise to forgiveness, and what forgiveness can entail. I want now to finish with some material on this that I covered in my book *Hauntings* (Frosh, 2013); the focus of the chapter in that book that I called "Forgiveness" is S. An-Sky's (1920) play, *The Dybbuk*, written between 1916 and 1920, and the remarkable film made of it in 1937 in Poland by Michał Waszyński. In the book, I point to the haunted nature of *The Dybbuk*, which of course is about possession by a dead spirit, and especially of the film. The world conjured by the film had already largely gone by the 1930s; but the faces and voices were real enough, as many of them belonged to the actual inhabitants of the village of Kazimierz, most of whom later died in the Nazi terror. The lead couple in the film survived, ironically and accidentally, when they missed their ship back to Poland from New York because of delays in making another film; and many of the other professional actors also fled to America. But the dominant musical presence in *The Dybbuk*, the great cantor Gershon Sirota, was killed in the Warsaw ghetto in 1943. Reading or watching the play, but particularly viewing the film, is thus itself an act of memory and resurrection, laced unbearably with the knowledge of what came next; haunted, that is, by the future more than by the past. "What was to come" is the temporality of viewing; the viewer's body is itself inhabited by the dybbuk of those whose lives were cut short, and perhaps have nowhere to go. Even in its *form*, then, *The Dybbuk* is a ghostly resurrection, something blowing back from before the Nazi Holocaust, back too toward the period of wonders and miracles that many Jews took refuge in during the time of the Hassidim, back also to the Chmielnicki[9] massacres of the seventeenth century, which are strongly referenced. It consequently embodies a kind of possession which is hard to lay to rest, however fervently the Kaddish, the Jewish memorial prayer, is recited, as it is at the end of the film. It is also a manifestation not only of the melancholic elements of destroyed cultures, returning again and again to trouble and distress the present, but of the call to restitution and possibly, though sometimes at extreme cost, to forgiveness.

The story of *The Dybbuk* can be stated briefly, though this does it an injustice: two men promise that their unborn babies will marry one another as a way to seal their own mutual devotion; when it comes to it, fate and human blindness block the marriage, and the erstwhile groom dies. He returns to possess his bride as a spirit or dybbuk; indeed, in a deviation from the conventional dybbuk story, he is welcomed by her. After a painful and dramatic trial and then exorcism by the rabbi, the dybbuk leaves the girl's body, but she wills herself to die in order to be reunited with him in death. The conventional formula on discovering a death—"Blessed be the true Judge"—is the final phrase of the play and film. My suggestion is that *The Dybbuk* recognizes how a society can desert its own symbolic promises. Or maybe one should think of it as showing how all social orders—all symbolic structures—are full of rifts and incompleteness, and what *The Dybbuk* dramatizes is how painful it is when one comes face to face with these. The lovers strive to heal this rift by fulfilling a pledge that has not been kept; they thereby affirm the well-being of the symbolic order, its phallic potency, just when the impossible dilemmas of that potency are visible to all, when it has betrayed them. Repairing the damage done by this betrayal is, however, impossible: It would involve a wedding between a dead groom and a living bride; it cannot be done without violence. The rabbi tries to deal with this by casting out the intrusive dybbuk, but this does not work, and what we are then exposed to is a haunting by something that cannot be contained within the usual parameters of the symbolic order. Put more bleakly, *The Dybbuk* is a demonstration of how desperately we strive to maintain the appearance of symbolic order when experience demonstrates, time and again, that this order is teetering on the edge of collapse. And this is not fiction. While the story of the lovers is an invented one, the film of *The Dybbuk* is a very material spirit, an actual visitation from beyond the grave. It not only "brings to life" what once existed; it also fills out the present with the beings of those who have gone "before their time." It is a restless piece that holds the future responsible for what was to come. It demands that those who have broken their promise are held to account; but it also conjures up a melancholic consciousness in which what has been lost and hidden is brought into awareness, precisely so that—whatever the consequences—it can be mourned. This, too, is a mode of forgiveness.

But there is also something else. In her meditation on social violence, Judith Butler (2009) draws upon the psychoanalytic, specifically Kleinian, idea that our capacity to be ethical subjects is measured by our ability to make good the damage we do. She identifies this as "a certain ethical practice … that seeks to preserve life better than it destroys it" (p. 177). I take the phrase "to preserve life better than it destroys it" as a vital one both for Judaism and for psychoanalysis. Every one of us has injuriousness within us and is tempted to express that in relation to others with whom we have contact and on whom we are likely to be dependent. Recognition of this tendency to violence, this temptation to destroy everything, leads to recognition of the responsibility we have to struggle against the temptation and to acknowledge what we have done when the struggle fails. This leads me to my final example, which comes from one of Emmanuel Levinas' (1968) "Talmudic Readings". "The Temptation of Temptation" deals with an especially provocative moment in the Talmud (Tractate Shabbat) where the rabbis are debating the line from Exodus 19, 17 reading, "And they stopped at the foot of the mountain …" This refers to the moment of the Revelation at Mount Sinai; the Israelites are encamped there awaiting the word of God. The people declare their willingness to hear and obey the Torah Law, before they know exactly what will be in it, an act of apparent free choice. But how free were they really? The Talmud is not too sure.

> Rav Abdima bar Hama bar Hasa has said: This teaches us that the Holy One, Blessed be He, inclined the mountain over them like a tilted tub and that He said: If you accept the Torah, all is well, if not, here will be your grave. Rav Aha bar Jacob said: That is a great warning concerning the Torah.… Resh Lakish taught: What does

the verse (Genesis 1:31) mean: "Evening came, then morning, it was the sixth day"? The definite article is not necessary. Answer: God had established a covenant with the works of the Beginning: If Israel accepts the Torah, you will continue to exist. If not, I will bring you back to chaos.

Levinas proceeds with his analysis of this passage and the section that follows it in a suitably Talmudic way, by commenting on the text line by line. It is not possible to follow this in detail here, but I want to pull one element out from his discussion, the issue of the draw toward violence. The mountain hovered over the people, threatening to crush them—they were literally "beneath the mountain." Levinas (1968, p. 37) notes that "The choice of the Jewish way of being, of the difficult freedom of being Jewish, would have been a choice between this way and death … In the beginning was violence." The first choice is a forced one, from which no one can step back, because if they do they cease to be human, they cease to stand in any kind of ethical relationship with themselves or with others. This is clearly a challenging reading as it suggests that the absence of choice in the acceptance of the frame of the Torah instantiates violence at the heart of religious and moral action. It is the relationship between freedom and violence that is the focus of the next section, ending with "If Israel accepts the Torah, you will continue to exist. If not, I will bring you back to chaos." This is how Levinas reads the apparent lack of free choice embedded in the threat, *existence or chaos*:

> The mountain turned upside down like a tub above the Israelites thus threatened the universe. God, therefore, did not create without concerning himself with the meaning of creation. Being has a meaning. The meaning of being, the meaning of creation, is to realize the Torah. The world is here so that the ethical order has the possibility of being fulfilled. The act by which the Israelites accept the Torah is the act which gives meaning to reality. To refuse the Torah is to bring being back to nothingness. … The unfortunate universe also had to accept its subordination to the ethical order, and Mount Sinai was for it the moment in which its "to be" or "not to be" was being decided. The refusal of the Israelites would have been the signal for the annihilation of the entire universe. (p. 41)

The mountain hovers over all of us; thinking about it as a "tub" does not quite capture the degree of threat involved. We are not being offered a bath in a gentle container; we are being offered the choice between existence and chaos. "Being has a meaning," Levinas asserts; this meaning is that of an ethical responsibility toward others that founds the human as a subject. "The world is here so that the ethical order has the possibility of being fulfilled." Without this ethical framing, there is nothing; when it fails, there is no rest, there is only constant suffering "between two worlds," as An-Sky (1920) puts it in the subtitle to his play. The psychology and philosophy of this are powerful enough, but the politics of it are also pronounced. Speaking mythologically and metaphorically, as perhaps one must when dealing with claims of such specificity and grandiosity, the survival of humanity depends on the construction of social orders that accept an ethical frame that does justice to the needs of others, finding space for everyone to be recognized as full subjects. This also requires recognition of the violence that lies at the edges of the social order and therefore of the protective movement of acknowledgment and reparation required to keep the further visitation of that violence at bay. This is not a matter of "free" choice, but it *is* a choice—it just happens, however, that the choice is between existence and chaos. "If you accept, all is well, if not, here will be your grave." There is plenty of evidence that this is a real choice; we often go for chaos and the grave. It is still an open question whether we are capable of making the other choice, the one with its roots in forgiveness, but both psychoanalysis and Judaism insist that we try.

Notes

1. *Kabbalah* refers generically here to the Jewish mystical tradition.
2. Although "Torah" can be used to refer to all sacred learning, here it is used in its more common sense as referring to the Five Books of Moses.
3. A parashah (plural, parashot) is a section of the Five Books of Moses read consecutively each week in the synagogue.
4. The names of three consecutive parashot, which literally mean "After death," "Speak," and "Holiness."
5. There is a myth that while Miriam was alive, a well of water accompanied the Israelites through their forty-year wanderings in the wilderness.
6. Rabbi Shlomo ben Yitzchak, the foremost Jewish medieval biblical commentator.

7. The *sefirot* are held to be the "vessels" created by God to hold the original divine "light"; the mystics claim that several of these *sefirot* cracked, dispersing the light and requiring human agency to recover them.

8. *Mitzvot* are technically religious commandments, but the term is also used to refer to "good deeds."

9. Bohdan Chmielnicki was a Cossack leader, still revered in the Ukraine, whose uprising against the Polish–Lithuanian Commonwealth in the mid-seventeenth century was accompanied by vicious anti-Semitic attacks and the deaths of tens of thousands of Jews.

References

An-Sky, S. (1920). The Dybbuk. In: *The Dybbuk and Other Writings*. D. Roskies (Ed.). New York: Schocken, 1992.

Benjamin, J. (2009). A relational psychoanalysis perspective on the necessity of acknowledging failure in order to restore the facilitating and containing features of the intersubjective relationship (the shared third). *International Journal of Psychoanalysis, 90*: 441–450.

Benjamin, W. (1940). Theses on the philosophy of history. In: *Illuminations*. London: Pimlico, 1999.

Bergmann, M. S. (2009). [Letter to the editor] On: Leaps of Faith: Is Forgiveness a Useful Concept? *International Journal of Psychoanalysis, 90*(3): 640.

Brecht, K. (1995). In the aftermath of Nazi-Germany: Alexander Mitscherlich and psychoanalysis—legend and legacy. *American Imago, 52*: 291–312.

Brecht, K., Friedrich, V., Hermanns, L. M., Kaminer, I. J., & Juelich, D. H. (Eds.) (1985). *Here Life Goes On in a Most Peculiar Way: Psychoanalysis Before and After 1933*. Hamburg, Germany: Kellner Verlag.

Butler, J. (2009). *Frames of War*. London: Verso.

Butler, J. (2012). *Parting Ways*. New York: Columbia University Press.

Chasseguet-Smirgel, J. (1987). Time's White Hair We Ruffle: Reflections on the Hamburg Congress. *International Review of Psycho-Analysis, 14*: 433–444.

Erlich, H. S., Erlich-Ginor, M., & Beland, H. (2009). Being in Berlin: A large group experience in the Berlin Congress. *International Journal of Psychoanalysis, 90*: 809–825.

Freud, S. (1916–17). *Introductory Lectures on Psycho-Analysis (Part III)*. *S. E., 15–16*: 241–463. London: Hogarth.

Freud, S. (1920g). *Beyond the Pleasure Principle*. *S. E., 18*: 1–64. London: Hogarth.

Frosh, S. (2005). *Hate and the Jewish Science: Anti-Semitism, Nazism and Psychoanalysis*. London: Palgrave.

Frosh, S. (2012). The re-enactment of denial. In: A. Gulerce (Ed.), *Re(con)figuring Psychoanalysis: Critical Juxtapositions of the Philosophical, the Sociohistorical and the Political*. London: Palgrave.

Frosh, S. (2013). *Hauntings: Psychoanalysis and Ghostly Transmissions*. London: Palgrave.

Kafka, J. S. (1988). On reestablishing contact. *Psychoanalysis & Contemporary Thought, 11*: 299–308.

Klein, M. (1955). The psychoanalytic play technique. In: *Envy and Gratitude and Other Works 1946–1963*. New York: Delta, 1975.

Levinas, E. (1968). The temptation of temptation. In E. Levinas *Nine Talmudic Readings*. Bloomington, Indiana: Indiana University Press, 1990.

Lutzky, H. (1989). Reparation and Tikkun: A comparison of the Kleinian and Kabbalistic concepts. *International Review of Psycho-Analysis, 16*: 449–458.

Moses, R., & Hrushovski-Moses, R. (1986). A form of group denial at the Hamburg Congress. *International Review of Psycho-Analysis, 13*: 175–180.

Opening Ceremony, 34th IPA Congress (1986). *International Journal of Psychoanalysis, 67*: 2–4.

Scholem, G. (1941). *Major Trends in Jewish Mysticism*. New York: Schocken.

Steiner, R. (2000). *It is a New Kind of Diaspora: Explorations in the Sociopolitical and Cultural Context of Psychoanalysis*. London: Karnac.

Weinshel, E. (1986). Report of the 34th International Psycho-Analytic Congress. *Bulletin of the International Psychoanalytical Association, 67*: 87–130.

Zornberg, A. (2015). *Bewilderments*. New York: Schocken.

CHAPTER THREE

Sigmund Freud, the Jewish body, and hysteria

Sander L. Gilman

Introduction

Many years ago, I was standing alongside my then two-year-old son who was examining himself in a full-length mirror before we were leaving the house together. He stared—he smiled—he moved around and posed—he was intrigued in the looking.

I watched this scene unfold and it elicited in me a series of imaginings. I imagined that our prior quite eventful two years together was collapsed into this moment of time. The totality of our interactions along with my unconscious images of him as well as those of his mother were being lived out in this brief opportunity of his viewing himself as if for the first time.

As vital as one's parents' unconscious representations of us are for our body images, it of course does not stop there. For my image of my son is born in part from my image of myself—which is shaped by that of my parents, and my wife's by her parents. And before them by their parents. And on and on like a mirror image of mirrors. Back in time to what we then call "culture."

We know this from psychoanalytic work. We also know this from empirical research. Recently there has been survey data that confirms these findings. For example, if you take a group of average weight children, some will have parents who view them accurately as being of average weight. These children will in turn grow into average weight teenagers. Some of these average weight children will have parents who nevertheless view them as overweight. Indeed, those children will grow into overweight teenagers. Parenting matters (Robinson & Sutin, 2016, p. 5).

The meanings of our bodies to all of us derive from the interaction between intrapsychic images and interpersonal/cultural conceptualizations.

The former, the intrapsychic meanings, allow for demonstration through clinical example. For instance, a middle-aged married woman whose analysis I supervised revealed that while in college in New York in the nineties she was involved with the early productions of The Vagina Monologues. During that time she was sexually very active with many and brief partners. Her analyst came to learn a great deal about the meanings to her of these activities. He and the patient came to know that the freedom that these behaviors ostensibly represented for her were more apparent than real. In the intimate setting of her love life and her analysis she in fact could not actually utter the word "vagina." Indeed, she became aware that apart from the exhibitionistic pride that she demonstrated in her public performances she felt a repugnance for her genitals and for her sexual self in general, which on occasion led to her mutilating herself.

Freud opened up the subject of our sexuality within the culture at large—hence the opportunity now for the public Vagina Monologues. More importantly, in addition Freud introduced a method whereby the intimate dimension of our sexuality and much else in our lives can be explored and one's childhood-related inhibitions and conflicts recognized and ameliorated.

In this woman's analysis she became able to distinguish her own body from that of her mother's from whom she had inadequately individuated even into her middle age. She also became able to recognize her own desires as well as the conflicts that were associated for her with those desires. This allowed her to become able to more quietly name her genitals and recognize the loveliness that was represented in her passions. Her sexuality—her body image—matured from one which had been limited by a brutal self-consciousness that objectified herself to herself. She became able instead to experience her self—her body—as a graceful vehicle for the expression of arousal and love.

This individual's body image was born from the unique contributions of her parents' unconscious life, her biologic predispositions, and the vagaries of her childhood. And yet culture also plays a part. We learn this for exam-ple from recent research that documents the difference between Eastern and Western family influences on children's developing body images.

In the West, negative body image comments by fathers have been shown to have a greater influence on their sons' sense of themselves than on their daughters' who are more influenced by comments from their mother. In contrast, in Eastern cultures, it is only comments by mothers that have been shown to influence the physical self-image of their children, both sons and daughters (Chng & Fassnacht, 2016, pp. 93–99).

In addition to parenting, culture matters.

All one needs to do to appreciate the impact of culture on the physical image of a people is to study the various ways that the body of the Jew has been represented throughout history. These anti-Semitic representations have included a focus on the foot of the Jew which in the Middle Ages was cast as akin to the devil's cloven hoof. Later, the supposed chronic infirmi-ties of the Jews led to their being deemed unsuitable as foot soldiers and hence placed outside the basic requirements of citizenship and the body politic at large.

The emphasis on the visual representation of the body—the body image—was a hallmark of the work of Charcot, the nineteenth-century neurologist who was a teacher of Freud. Sander Gilman has described how Charcot was no stranger to the European anti-Semitism that was endemic at that time in academic and medical circles. The Jew had been seen as the embodiment of the feminized man—the male hysteric. Charcot's emphasis on the external visual representation, the satirized body image of the cartooned Jew, was a precursor to Freud's more nuanced recognition of the internal life of the individual. Not how one appears but how one imagines.

As Gilman describes in his book The Jew's Body (1991), Freud advanced beyond Charcot's way of seeing. Instead of simply viewing the surface, Freud's eyes identified the presence of internal psychological conflict in the etiology of hysteria. The feminized Jew disease—hysteria—became a window into the unconscious life of all humans. Freud advanced our think-ing from the surface to the depth, from the exterior to the interior, from the generic to the particular.

Our attention to the topic of the body image alerts us to the defensive-ness, the superficiality, in focusing on the image of one's body. Body image represents our image of our body. This is in contrast to a sense of one's animated experience of our body—a lived body, a body containing desire, distress, and possibility. A body in relation to the external world not to its visage in a mirror.

This topic presses upon us all these days as we further immerse ourselves in our body images as represented in digital media. We take selfies, send Instagram and Facebook messages depicting ourselves. Our body images preoccupy us all.

This subject has particular weight for many of us in the mental health professions now that Skype psychotherapy is increasingly commonplace. We struggle to come to terms with both its advantages and limitations. We have much to learn about the meanings associated with relating to an "other" through their image on a screen. For many, the lowered sense of presence that the Skype image of their body makes available to their analyst reproduces the self-alienation that is so common a problem for many patients.

The analytic journey of the patient mentioned earlier entailed her coming to inhabit her actual body, with its imperfections and desires. This allowed her to shed to a large degree her obsession with her image of her body that had existed in her mind merely as a stimulator of others. She was enabled to live in her authentic experience of her physicalness that came alive as the imperfect container for her history and her motherhood.

Harvey Schwartz

* * *

One of the most extraordinary moments in the history of medicine occurs when the young neurologist Sigmund Freud, newly returned from a post-doctoral stay in Paris studying with the preeminent neurologist of the day Jean-Martin Charcot, speaks to the medical establishment in Vienna about the non-gendered nature of hysterical symptoms. Freud's initial presentation of his work on hysteria in Vienna was a paper on male hysteria— not the Jewish male predisposition for hysteria but on the universal male potential for hysteria. Freud's overt argument was evidently (the paper is lost) that men, too, suffer from hysteria as the etiology of the disease was not in the gender of the patient but in the patient's traumatic experiences. It is well known that Freud, in the autobiographical account he wrote of the occasion some forty years after the event, recalled the "bad reception" which this paper on male hysteria had when he presented it before the Viennese

Society of Physicians on October 15, 1886.[1] Freud's powerful memory was that his hearers thought that what he "said was incredible. ... One of them, an old surgeon, actually broke out with the exclamation: 'But, my dear sir, how can you talk such nonsense? *Hysteron* [sic] means the uterus. So how can a man be hysterical?'" (Freud, 1925d, p. 15).[2] Freud's angry memory was aimed at the narrow-minded claim of this old man, representing the Viennese medical establishment, that it, and it alone, had command of Greek. Here the Jewish psychoanalyst placed his claim to control a discourse of academic culture. Freud's memory was certainly shaped by the hostile reception which psychoanalysis had gotten in the four decades following his talk. Psychoanalysis was seen as a Jewish pseudo-science and as a form of mass hysteria, a "psychic epidemic among physicians."[3] Freud laughs at the "old surgeon" who claims to understand culture but whose very inability to command its language disqualifies him from it.

It was the young, French-trained Freud who knew that the concept of hysteria was tied to universals (which, at that point, he thought of as having their origin in trauma) and was not merely a reflex of the biological uniqueness of a subgroup. It was hysteria (the hallmark of the new science) that Freud wished to rescue from the crabbed claws of a Viennese medical establishment which could not even get its Greek correct, for *hustera* is the correct form of the Greek noun for uterus. Thus the young Jew (and Freud understood himself from his exposure to the virulent "scientific" anti-Semitism of the Viennese University as a Jew) showed his command over not only the language of science (represented by Charcot's discourse on hysteria) but also the language of culture (Greek). Freud's sense, like that of his contemporaries, was that hysteria did not manifest itself as a disease of the womb but of the imagination. It was a functional illness resulting from trauma, rather than the result of inheritance, as he had shown in his paper on heredity and inheritance. And with the claim that male hysteria existed, he attempted to free the other group targeted, women, from their special risk. This did not absolve the female from being the group most at risk, however, for the idea of a pathological human imagination structurally replaced the image of the floating womb as the central etiology of hysteria. And women's imagination was understood by the physicians of the time, such as Paul Julius Möbius (1901), as diseased. What was removed from the category of hysteria as Freud brought it back to Vienna was its insistence on another group, the Jews, as the group which essentially replaced the woman as at risk.

In the actual contemporary record of the discussion following Freud's paper, attributed to the young Austrian-Jewish physician-writer Arthur Schnitzler (1988, pp. 75–80), there is a further complication[4]. Not only is there no mention of the impossibility of male hysteria, but Theodor Meynert as well as Moritz Rosenthal claim that, while less frequent than female hysteria, cases were well documented in the various Viennese hospitals as well as in the German medical literature. Heinrich von Bamberger, who was in the chair at the meeting, commented further that while he certainly had seen cases of male hysteria, he was troubled by Freud's claim that his case was only the result of trauma. Indeed, he noted, the very case Freud cites, "shows a hereditary predisposition" for the disease. Not trauma, which is the result of accident, but heredity, which cannot be altered, is the source of male hysteria, according to Bamberger. Thus, within the very concept of hysteria as Freud elaborated it, the question of the hysteric's heredity and predisposition was hotly contested.

The impact of such fantasies of the biological nature of the Jew, the Jew's body, his psyche, his soul, on the development of psychoanalysis is clear. The special nature of the Jew, the diseases and sociopathic acts ascribed to it, are a universal in the general culture of the time. It is no surprise that the Jew is seen in terms of this dominant paradigm of the late nineteenth century as this age saw the biologization of all arenas of culture. We find Jewish biological and medical scientists of the day forced to deal with, what is for them, the unstated central epistemological problem of late nineteenth-century biological science: How one could be the potential subject of a scientific study at the same time that one had the role of the observer; how one could be the potential patient at the same moment one was supposed to be the physician. This was especially a problem in Vienna, where the domination of the so-called "second Viennese school" stressed the central role of the physician as scientist and the independent, neutral role of the physician-scientist as diagnostician. It is the striving of the neutral, the universal, for the overarching explanation which provides the rationale for the scientist-physician's gaze in the world of Viennese academic medicine.

And that science saw the Jew as the sufferer from hysteria. Maurice Fishberg's *The Jews: A Study of Race and Environment* (1911) states the case boldly: "The Jews, as is well known to every physician, are notorious sufferers of the functional disorders of the nervous system. Their nervous organization is constantly under strain, and the least injury will disturb its smooth workings" (p. 6).[5] The origin of this predisposition is neither consanguineous marriage ("the modern view ... [is that they] are not at all detrimental to the health of the offspring") nor the occupations of the Jew ("hysteria [is] ... met with in the poorer classes of Jews ... as well as in the richer classes") (Fishberg, 1904, p. 225). It is the result of the urban concentration of the Jews and "the repeated persecutions and abuses to which the Jews were subjected during the two thousand years of the Diaspora" (ibid.). These influences, found at the *fin de siècle* primarily among Eastern Jews, according to Fishberg show the predisposition of these specific groups of Jews to illnesses such as hysteria: "Organic as well as functional derangements of the nervous system are transmitted hereditarily from one generation to another" (ibid.). It is not *all* Jews who are hysterics, but Eastern Jews, and primarily Eastern male Jews, according to Fishberg: "The Jewish population of [Warsaw] alone is almost exclusively the inexhaustible source for the supply of specimens of hysterical humanity, particularly the hysteria in the male, for all the clinics of Europe" (1911, pp. 324–325). Here the American Jew Fishberg misquotes the French psychiatrist Fulgence Raymond, who had stated (1889, p. 71) that Jews of Warsaw formed a major sector of the mentally ill of that city.[6] It is Fishberg's misquote of Raymond which becomes the standard view in German psychiatry, as quoted, for example, in Hugo Hoppe (1903, p. 26). It appears within Freud's circle when Isidor Sadger noted at the November 11, 1908 meeting of the Vienna Psychoanalytic Society: "In certain races (Russian and Polish Jews), almost every man is hysterical."[7] It is the male Jew from the East, from the provinces, who is most at risk for hysteria.

This view had been espoused by Charcot, who diagnosed on February 19, 1889 the case of a Hungarian Jew named Klein, "a true child of Ahasverus," as a case of male hysteria. Klein had a hysterical contracture of the hand and an extended numbness of the right arm and leg. It is the limping of the Jew which Charcot stressed. Klein "wandered sick and limping on foot to Paris" where he arrived on December 11, 1888. He appeared at the Salpêtrière the next day, "his feet so bloody that he could not leave his bed for many days." Klein "limped at the very beginning of his illness." Charcot reminded his listeners that the patient "is a Jew and that he has already revealed his pathological drives by his wanderings." His "travel-mania" could be seen in the fact that "as soon as he was on his feet again, he wanted to go to Brazil" (Charcot, 1887, pp. 347–353).[8] Wandering and limping mark the hysterical Jew as diseased, and diseased because of intermarriage. This theme is elaborated in the work of Charcot's last major student, Henry Meige, who writes his dissertation (1893) on these "wandering Jews," seeing them as the con-temporary incarnation of the legendary Wandering Jew. In his thesis he reproduces their portraits so that one can study their physiognomy for the signs of their hysteria.[9]

The hysteria of the male Jew, especially the Eastern Jew, remains a truism of medical science through the decades. Prof. Hermann Strauss of the Jewish Hospital in Berlin, in one of the most cited studies of the pathology of the Jews, provides a bar chart representing the risk of the Jews for hysteria (1927, p. 35). Here the relationship between men and women indicates that male Jews suffer twice as often from hysteria than do male non-Jews. The standard textbooks of the period reflect this view. While it is clear that women are still the predominant sufferers from the disease, it is evident from the visual representation of the cases of hysteria that there is a clear "feminization" of the male Jew in the context of the occurrence of hysteria. This view is paralleled by the findings in the United States that "in European races, melancholic or depressive types of mental disorder are most frequent amongst the Germanic and Scandinavian peoples" (Bannister & Hektoen, 1888, p. 464).

The liberal-Jewish neurologist, Moriz Benedikt (1895), professor of neurology at the University of Vienna at the *fin de siècle*, also linked the "American" quality of life with the appearance of hysteria—a disease which is accepted by him as "a uniquely feminine nervous disease"—in men. (It is remarkable that only Jewish physicians in Vienna dealt with the question of male hysteria before Freud, as well as Freud himself.) It is the struggle for life in the city which causes the madness of the male Jew. According to Cecil F. Beadles: "Mental anxiety and worry are the most frequent causes of mental breakdown. They are all excitable and live excitable lives, being constantly under the high pressure of business in town" (1900, p. 736). The reason for this inability to cope with the stresses of modern life lies in "heredi-tary influences," that is, in their being Jews (Hyde, 1901–02, p. 470).[10] And their "Jewishness" is a sign of their being out of their correct space. For they are ill, "like many orientals (e.g., Mohammedans) who have a disposition to hysteria" (Weygandt, 1902, p. 32).

Benedikt needs to argue against the equation of race and madness (1901, pp. 503–509). For the "insanity of the Jew" is one of the risks which all Jews would have to face. In a detailed answer to Beadles, he presents a convo-luted and complex argument about the special status of the nervousness of the Jew. He accepts the reality of Beadle's charge. It is, however, a quality over which "evolution has no power … [and] which is deeply rooted in the organism." Benedickt counters this by arguing against the uniformity of the Jews as a race and sees the origin of the mental illness of the Jews in the external social pressures "in times of exile, dispersion, and persecution." The Jews are not really even a nation, for "the first condition necessary for a nation is a common language." "Other nations could find an outlet for their passions and emotions in outward actions; the Jews found an outlet for them usually at the expense of health, and so became more and more neurotic." This neurosis resulted in "excessive sexual intercourse, *intra matrimonium*" and caused the "hysterical aphonia, in endemic form … [which] are very frequent in Jews, male and female." This has caused "neurologists all over the world [to be] interested in the number, intensity, and variety of cases seen amongst the Jews." The lost language of the Jews, the inability to speak any tongue flawlessly, marks the Jews as ill. But what does Benedikt see as the cause of the madness of the Jews? The "ill-treatment and cruelty to … which they have been subjected." This even explains to him why Jews, who have a lower incidence of "syphilis and drunkenness," also have a higher rate of general paralysis. For it is therefore clear that syphilis cannot be the cause of the general paralysis of the insane, luetic tabes. Rather it is the result of social factors. With acculturation new nervous diseases afflict the Jews. Jewish women, "formerly pampered neurotic individuals," now became "eccentric.… Very many of them became, by reason of superficial learning, actually perverse." "They quickly entered into the modern economic contest with all its fatal consequences as regards nervous integrity." Benedikt's model, as is clear from all of his examples, is the Eastern Jew, hampered by his ghetto experience (1918, pp. 266–270).[11] And it is Yiddish which for Benedikt is the marker of Jewish mental illness: The "so-called" language, with its coarse gestures, seems to have a magical quality which prevents the acculturation of the Eastern Jews and which prolongs their risk for mental illnesses. Indeed, Theodor Reik pointed out that Eastern Jews communicated as much with "gestures and … facial expressions, the rise and fall of the voice of the story-teller" as with words (1962, pp. 33–34).

Sigmund Freud struggles with this notion of predisposition in his pivotal paper on "Heredity and the Aetiology of the Neuroses," first written and published in French in 1896, in which he attempted to dislodge this understanding of a social trauma as the origin of hysteria. This paper marked his break with Jean-Martin Charcot (who had died three years earlier) and Charcot's view that hysteria was an inherited phenomenon. Freud dismissed the primacy of the inherited disposition for hysteria (such as attributed by Charcot to the Jews). He stressed the difference between a "similar heredity" which always produces the same diseases with the same signs and symptoms (such as Huntington's chorea) and those diseases with a "dissimilar heredity," which produce seemingly unrelated illness with a myriad of signs and symptoms (1896a, p. 145). For the latter sources other than inheritance must be sought. In his search for the etiology of such psychopathologies, Freud further distinguished between "preconditions" (i.e., heredity) and "specific causes" of a disease. Both are necessary to create similar disease profiles, while the more general "concurrent causes" are sufficient but not necessary. Freud employed the model of the continuum which he used in his model of "bisexuality"—he sees "preconditions" and "specific causes" on a spectrum; as one decreases in importance, the other increases. It is the totality which produces the illness, just as the individual may be more or less male or female, the totality making up the entire personality structure.

Freud dismissed as marginal all of those "concurrent causes" which had been used to explain the existence of neurosis (in Jews as well as others): "emotional disturbance, physical exhaustion, acute illness, intoxications, traumatic accidents, intellectual overwork, etc." (p. 148). Thus he also rejected the claim that psychopathologies such as neurasthenia are the "fruits of our modern civilization." He found the roots of these neuroses in early sexual experience: "These functional pathological modifications *have as their common source the subject's sexual life, whether they lie in a disorder of his contemporary sexual life or in important events in his past life*" (p. 149, emphasis in original). Freud makes these "sexual disorders" the primary cause of neuroses; heredity is a peripheral cause.

Freud proposes two sets of differential diagnoses: He distinguished between neurasthenia, the product of masturbation or "a sexual constitution analogous to what is brought about in a neurasthenic as a result of masturbation" and anxiety neurosis, the result of "abstinence, unconsummated genital excitation … coition which is imperfect or interrupted … sexual efforts which exceed the subject's psychical capacity, etc." (pp. 150–151). He also differentiated between hysteria and obsessional neurosis: the former caused by "some event of the subject's sexual life appropriate for the production of a distressing emotion"; the latter caused by such "an event which has given pleasure" (p. 155). The pleasure in the sexual act is different for the male and for the female: For the male pleasure is the result of the aggressive desire of experienced sexuality; for the female, the enjoyment is generated by the sexual act.

Both hysteria and obsessional neurosis are caused by real events, remembered physical contact with the child's genitalia. Hysteria is the result of "passive sexuality, an experience submitted to with indifference or with a small degree of annoyance or fright" (p. 155). This event is real to the sufferer, not as an event in the past, but "... *as though it were a contemporary event*" (p. 154, emphasis in original). The living of a life in the present which has been marked by trauma in the past (either the past of the individual or the group) is the basic explanatory model for the present state of the difference of the Jews. Thus, Freud concludes, what appears to be hereditary in the acute symptoms of patients, such as the occurrence of "a pair of neurotic patients" in the same family, proves to be a "pair of little lovers in their earliest childhood—the man suffering from obsessions and the woman from hysteria. If they are brother and sister, one might mistake for a result of nervous heredity what is in fact the consequence of precocious experience" (p. 156). Here Freud has gendered the differential diagnosis—the female is passive or frightened; the male feels pleasure.

Yet Freud's dismissal of heredity as the cause of the neurosis provides a rationale for restructuring the concept of trauma, removing it from the world of daily life and centering it in the world of the sexual. Jews no longer will suffer from such symptoms of neurasthenia as "flatulent dyspepsia, constipation, or sexual weakness" (p. 150). (to list only a few of the traditional "Jewish" symptoms which appear on Freud's list of neurasthenic symptoms) purely because of their heredity, but because of sexual practices, such as masturbation, which are universal rather than particularistically Jewish. By moving hysteria to the realm of the incestuous, Freud eliminates the trauma of circumcision, the most evident "*precocious experience of sexual relations with actual excitement of the genitals, resulting from sexual abuse committed by another person*" from the etiology of neurosis (p. 152, emphasis in original). Circumcision is clearly understood as "frightening" within much of the medical literature opposed to it and within the complicated literature on *metsitsah* during the *fin de siècle*. Incest, especially brother–sister incest, is yet another charge brought regularly against the Jews as the etiology for specific forms of somatic and mental illnesses. But it is the removal of circumcision from the category of the causative factors for mental illness by dismissing the arguments about the heredity of mental illness (or its disposition) and the stress on the specific nature of sexual trauma, as opposed to other traumatic factors, which lies at the heart of Freud's final dismissal of Charcot and Charcot's model of hysteria. Freud's view was clearly a minority voice, as C. H. Hughes noted about Freud's paper on "The Aetiology of Hysteria" (1896a): "Hysteria, whatever its exciting causes, whether in the premature or over sexual, grief, disappointment or other psychoneural sources of depression and exhausting excitation, is usually bad neuropathic endowment, dormant at birth but ready—prepared like the lucifer match—for flame when rightly struck. Herr Sigmond [sic] Freud should try again" (Kiell, 1988, p. 36).

And he does try again. In 1897 Freud abandoned his trauma theory of neurosis. He realized that it was not the specific experiences of a select (but extensive) group of individuals whom Freud was treating, but rather a reflex of human development which he was seeing. He was observing the results of the fantasy of maltreatment rather than maltreatment itself. Freud separated these two moments though continuing to see a linkage between the empirical and fantasy in his own empirical studies on fantasy. Freud simultaneously elides and displaces the distinction between real events and fantasy. Freud's position was that of the racial biologist who saw the factors of Jewish identity as signs of the racial nature of the Jews. It is unimportant whether these qualities are understood as "inherited" (i.e., congenital) or "acquired" (but now an aspect of the genotype). Through this mechanism Freud hopes to free Jews, such as himself and his father, from the charge of being diseased, of lying, of being corrupt and corrupting.

In 1895, Freud evolved a four-fold formula to describe the origin of neurosis, based on Aristotle's four-fold analysis of causality. Needed was 1) a precondition, 2) specific cause, 3) concurrent cause, and 4) precipitating cause (1895b, pp. 135–136). The precondition was the existing disposition to disease, a disposition either acquired or innate. The specific causes, such as the seduction of the child, lead to the specific symptom formation, like the *globus hystericus*. The "concurrent causes," such as overwork or exhaustion, are seen as less important but as having a contributory role in the appearance of the neurosis. The actual precipitating cause was simply the final trigger which occurred before the symptoms became evident.

This model was certainly sufficient to explain the mental illnesses of the Jews. The precondition was either the inheritance of the Jews or precipitating diseases such as syphilis; the specific cause, the "2000 years of oppression," the concurrent cause, the "overwork" and "stresses of civilization," and whatever individual precipitating cause could be found in each individual case.

But Freud needed to discount the role of degeneracy, of "pathogenic heredity," as it "left no room for the acquisition of nervous disease" (1893a, p. 23). It also meant that all Jews, including Sigmund Freud, were at risk for specific forms of mental illness. His answer was to see the inheritance of trauma, following a Lamarckian model, as the source of disease, rather than some vague "Jewish predisposition to mental illness." What was originally sufficient (the specific cause) became necessary in Freud's revision of the etiology of neurosis. Trauma becomes the cause of neurosis.

Once "real" seduction is abandoned as the source of hysteria, and the source of neurosis is seen as lying in the fantasy of the oedipal struggle, then the reality of this model is drawn into question. In order to universalize the Jewish physical predisposition for illness, Freud evolved his own theory of the relationship between constitution and neurosis. He developed the law of the etiological complemental series, the idea that constitution and trauma complement one another: The weaker the constitution, the less the trauma needed to create a neurosis. Seeking after the meaning of trauma, Freud restructured his presentation of the etiology of neurosis. In the *Introductory Lectures on Psycho-Analysis* (1916–17), Freud stressed the etiological significance of 1) hereditary (and primal) dispositions, 2) infantile impressions, and 3) adult experiences (p. 362). It is in the clinical significance of phylogeny as a universal source of the predisposition to neurosis that Freud remains adamant. "Real" trauma lies in the universal past of all human beings, not solely in the Jewish experience in the Diaspora.[12] Here degeneracy is abandoned and the inheritance of acquired characteristics becomes a means of moving the Jews into the mainstream of the neurosis.

On December 5, 1906, this topic came up for discussion at the Viennese Psychoanalytic Society following a paper on Wilhelm Stekel's theory of the origin of nervousness. Isidor Sadger commented "on the widespread occurrence of nervousness (especially obsessional neurosis and hysteria) among the Polish Jews."[13] The cause of this is the "Jew's addiction to rumination ... [which] has been characteristic of them for thousands of years." It is the inheritance of specific forms of a "common mental construction" which lies at the heart of the Jew's predisposition to mental illness.[14] The view that the Eastern Jew was essentially at risk for hysteria permeated even the discussion of this circle of mainly Eastern European Jews, transplanted to Vienna. They saw, not themselves at risk, but "those" Eastern Jews, an abstraction which they distanced from their own persona.

In Charcot's clinic there was an often-stated assumption that Jews, especially Jews from the East, were at great risk for mental illness (see Goldstein, 1987). This view was shared in the general culture of the time. Following the collapse of the Catholic Union Generale Bank in 1882, there was a great rise in public anti-Semitism. In the spring of 1886, as a result Eduoard Drumont's best-seller, *La France juive* appeared, perhaps the most important French anti-Semitic tractate. Drumont cited psychological statistics to show that Jews, especially Jews from the East, were most at risk for mental illness, and therefore presented a social danger to the French body politic. And he cited statements made by Charcot "in his lectures in the Salpêtrière" quite directly (vol. 1, pp. 105–106).[15]

No wonder that Jewish scientists such as Jacobs, Fishberg, and Freud— in very different ways—sought to find the hysteric outside of their own immutable self-image. For that image was within the biology of race. This consistency of character, with its deviant sexual nature, leads to the disease which marks the Jew—hysteria. The etiology of the Jew's hysteria, like the hysteria of the woman, was to be sought in "sexual excess" (Beadles, 1900, p. 732). Specifically in the "incestuous" inbreeding of this endogenous group: "Being very neurotic, consanguineous marriages among Jews cannot but be detrimental to the progeny" (Fishberg, 1904, p. 349). And the converse is also true: "The excessive tendency to the neuroses [among] … the Jews, [results] from their mode of life and consanguineous marriages through long centuries" (Clarke, 1894, p. 150).[16] Jews (especially male Jews) are sexually different; they are hysterical and their gaze reveals it.

Race is but one category in the visualization of the hysteric, the construction of which took many different forms. A composite image of the hysteric was revealed in bits and snatches, one that seemed to reveal the "truth" about the hysteric's difference to an onlooker.

In the course of the 1890s Freud abandoned much of the work of the anti-Semitic Charcot[17]—for whom Jews, as the essential "moderns," were at special risk as hysterics—and entered his new alliance with the provincial Jew Hippolyte Bernheim (Morgan, 1989, pp. 268–272). Much of this is worked out in Freud's French-language paper on the meaning of heredity for the etiology of hysteria (1896a). Such a movement is paralleled to the abandonment of ideas of trauma—still for Charcot the cause of hysteria (in women as well as in Jews) and its replacement with the etiology of hysteria in the psyche. As Freud states:

For [the physician] will be able to convince himself of the correctness of the assertions of the school of Nancy [Bernheim] at any time on his patients, whereas he is scarcely likely to find himself in a position to confirm from his own observation the phenomena described by Charcot as "major hypnotism," which seem only to occur in a few sufferers from *grande hysterie*. (1889a, p. 98)

It is the scientific "observation," the gaze of the Jew rather than the gaze directed at the Jew, which marks the distinction between Bernheim and Charcot. Freud's "conversion" to Bernheim's mode of seeing the "usual" rather than seeing the "unique" also marks the beginning of his rejection of reducing the origin of hysteria to the single, traumatic event.

But what does "trauma" mean? One meaning relates it to the debate about congenital circumcision and the inheritance of acquired character-istics. To trace the meaning of trauma means seeing the reason the Eastern European Jew appears as a hysteric (or perhaps more accurately, the provin-cial Jew as parvenu, out of his mind because he is out of his natural place). It is the discourse on the relationship between "trauma" and "hysteria" which provides the key to Freud's—and many of his contemporaries'—ambivalence concerning models for therapy.

All human beings become inventors of their own past. All trauma is part of the universal experience of growth and development. The Jews' rationale that their illness is the result of two thousand years of persecution becomes no more important than any other claims of trauma. It ends the inheri-tance of the acquired trauma of Jewish experience and makes it part of the origin of that which makes all human beings human. In the famous let-ter of September 21, 1897 Freud admitted to Fliess, "I no longer believe in my neurotica ..." (Masson, 1985, pp. 264–266). For believing in the reality of trauma would mean "... in all cases, the *father*, not excluding my own, had to be accused of being perverse." Freud abandoned a system which demands mimetic, psychic representation of reality for one which sees the psyche as the place for the play of fantasy. He abandoned the act of seeing difference. And yet he clearly never abandoned the status of science asso-ciated with that manner of seeing. For as much as Freud was aware of the problems of positivistic epistemology, the status of the scientific gaze over-came his sense of its limitations.

Notes

1. This is the "myth" which Frank Sulloway, in *Freud: Biologist of the Mind* (1979, p. 592) wishes to identify as "Myth One," the primal myth, in Freud's falsification of his own history. It is clear that this (and the other "myths") are fascinating insights into Freud's understanding of his own career and provide the material for interpretation, not censure.

2. On the background and meaning of male hysteria see Micale (1990, pp. 363–411). Micale does not link the question of the gender specificity of hysteria to that of race.

3. See the comments by the neurologists Theodor Sommers and Alfred Hoche quoted in the *Psychiatrisch-Neurologische Wochenschrift, 12* (1910): 128.

4. There are other accounts of this talk which supplement this report, see Sulloway (1979, p. 38).

5. Compare Fishberg's statement in "Nervous Diseases" (1904, vol. 9, p. 225): "Some physicians of large experience among Jews have even gone so far as to state that most of them are neurasthenic and hysterical."

6. "La population israélite fournit à elle seule presque tout le contingent des hystériques mâles" (Raymond, 1889, p. 71).

7. Protokolle der Wiener Psychoanalytischen Vereinigung, 2, p. 40; translation from Minutes of the Vienna Psychoanalytic Society, 2, p. 44.

8. J.-M. Charcot (1887), Leçons du Mardi a la Salpêtrière, 2, pp. 347–353; see the translation of the Poliklinische Vorträge, 2, pp. 299–304.

9. Henry Meige, Étude sur certains néuropathes voyageurs: Le juif-errant à la Salpêtrière (1893). On Meige and this text see Goldstein (1985). See the images and the discussion in Gilman (1991, pp. 60–103).

10. On the statistical background to the shift between the primarily German-Jewish population and the huge influx of Eastern European Jews into the United States see Billings (1890, p. 23). This is based on a questionaire sent to 15,000 and responses received from 10,618 Jewish families (60,630 persons), whose names had been obtained from "rabbis and presidents of congregations." This study showed that 227 Jews (116 men; 111 women) had died of "diseases of the nervous system" (including mental diseases: 18 men; 17 women) between 1885 and 1889. The "Jews have suffered a relatively greater loss than their neighbors by deaths from … disease of the nervous system … than the other peoples with whom they are compared" (p. 15). This report was condensed and published in a "popular" version as "Vital Statistics of the Jews" (1891).

11. This is also a detailed attack on Rafael Becker's Zionist explanation of the mental illness of the Jews.

12. On the discussion of Jewish experience after the Shoah and the reintroduction of the question of trauma, see Felman and Laub, (1992).

13. Protokolle der Wiener Psychoanalytischen Vereinigung, 1, p. 70; translation from Minutes of the Vienna Psychoanalytic Society, 1, p. 73.

14. Protokolle der Wiener Psychoanalytischen Vereinigung, 1, p. 93; translation from Minutes of the Vienna Psychoanalytic Society, 1, p. 98.

15. On the complicated issue of the structure of this argument and the Jewish response in the German-speaking lands, see Gilman, *Difference and Pathology* (1985, pp. 150–162).

16. Freud cites this volume in "Obsessions and Phobias" (1895c, p. 74).

17. See the discussion in Gilman, 1985, pp. 150–162. See also Chevalier (1985, pp. 45–50).

References

Bannister, H. M., & Hektoen, L. (1888). Race and insanity. *American Journal of Insanity, 44*: 456–470.

Beadles, C. F. (1900). The insane Jew. *Journal of Mental Science, 46*: 732, 736.

Benedikt, M. (1895). Die Seelenkunde des Menschen als reine Erfahrungswissenschaft. Leipzig, Germany: O. R. Reisland.

Benedikt, M. (1901). The insane Jew. An open letter to Dr. C. F. Beadles. *Journal of Mental Science, 47*: 503–509.

Benedikt, M. (1918). Der geisteskranke Jude. *Nord und Süd, 167*: 266–270.

Billings, J. S. (1890). Vital statistics of the Jews in the United States. *Census Bulletin, 19*: 23.

Charcot, J.-M. (1887). Leçons du Mardi a la Salpêtrière, 2. Paris: Aux bureaux du Progrès medical.

Chevalier, Y. (1985). Freud et l'antisemitisme—jalousie. *Amitié judéo-chretienne de France, 37*: 45–50.

Chng, S. C. W., & Fassnacht, D. B. (2016). Parental comments: Relationship with gender, body dissatisfaction, and disordered eating in Asian young adults. *Body Image, 16*(3): 93–99.

Clarke, J. M. (1894). Hysteria and neurasthenia. *Brain, 17*: 118–178.

Drumont, E. (1886). *La France juive: Essai d'histoire contemporaine, 2 vols.* Paris: C. Marpon et E. Flammarion.

Felman, S., & Laub, D. (1992). *Testimony: Crises of Witnessing in Literature, Psychoanalysis, and History.* New York: Routledge.

Fishberg, M. (1904). Nervous diseases. In: *The Jewish Encyclopedia, 12 vols.* New York: Funk & Wagnalls.

Fishberg, M. (1911). *The Jews: A Study of Race and Environment.* New York: Walter Scott.

Freud, S. (1889a). Review of August Forel's *Hypnotism. S. E., 1*: 98. London: Hogarth.

Freud, S. (1893a). On the psychical mechanism of hysterical phenomena: preliminary communication. *S. E., 3*: 23. London: Hogarth.

Freud, S. (1895b). On the grounds for detaching a particular syndrome from neurasthenia under the description "anxiety neurosis". *S. E., 3*: 135–136. London: Hogarth.

Freud, S. (1895c). Obsessions and phobias. *S. E., 3*: 74. London: Hogarth.

Freud, S. (1896a). Heredity and the aetiology of the neuroses. *S. E., 3*: 145–156. London: Hogarth.

Freud, S. (1916–17). Introductory Lectures on Psycho-Analysis. *S. E., 15–16*: 362. London: Hogarth.

Freud, S. (1925d). *An Autobiographical Study. S. E., 20*: 15. London: Hogarth.

Gilman, S. L. (1985). *Difference and Pathology: Stereotypes of Sexuality, Race, and Madness.* Ithaca, NY: Cornell University Press.

Gilman, S. L. (1991). *The Jew's Body.* London: Routledge, 2016.

Goldstein, J. (1985). The Wandering Jew and the problem of psychiatric anti-Semitism in fin-de-siècle France. *Journal of Contemporary History, 20*: 521–552.

Goldstein, J. (1987). *Console and Classify: the French Psychiatric Profession in the Nineteenth Century.* New York: Cambridge University Press.

Hoppe, H. (1903). Krankheiten und Sterblichkeit bei Juden und Nichtjuden. Berlin: S. Calvary.

Hyde, F. G. (1901–02). Notes on the Hebrew insane. *American Journal of Insanity, 58*: 470.

Kiell, N. (Ed.) (1988). *Freud without Hindsight: Reviews of His Works (1893–1939).* Madison, CT: International Universities Press.

Masson, J. M. (Ed.) (1985). *The Complete Letters of Sigmund Freud to Wilhelm Fliess, 1887–1904.* Cambridge, MA: Harvard University Press.

Meige, H. (1893). Étude sur certains néuropathes voyageurs: Le juif-errant à la Salpêtrière. Paris: L. Battaille.

Micale, M. (1990). Charcot and the idea of hysteria in the male: Gender, mental science, and medical diagnosis in late nineteenth-century France. *Medical History, 34*: 363–411.

Möbius, P. J. (1901). Über den physiologischen Schwachsinn des Weibes. Halle, Germany: Marhold. (Eighth edition, 1908.)

Morgan, W. G. (1989). Freud's lithograph of Charcot: A historical note. *Bulletin of the History of Medicine, 63*: 268–272.

Raymond, F. (1889). L'Étude des Maladies du Système Nerveux en Russie. Paris: O. Doin.

Reik, T. (1962). *Jewish Wit.* New York: Gamut Press.

Robinson, E., & Sutin, A. R. (2016). Parental perception of weight status and weight gain across childhood. *Pediatrics, 137*: 5.

Schnitzler, A. (1988). Medizinische Schriften.H. Thomé (Ed.). Vienna: Paul Zsolnay.

Strauss, H. (1927). Erkrankungen durch Alkohol und Syphilis bei den Juden. *Zeitschrift für Demographie und Statistik der Juden, 4*: 33–39.

Sulloway, F. (1979). *Freud, Biologist of the Mind: Beyond the Psychoanalytic Legend.* New York: Basic Books.

Vital Statistics of the Jews (1891). *North American Review, 153*: 70–84.

Weygandt, W. (1902). *Atlas und Grundriss der Psychiatrie.* Munich, Germany: J. F. Lehmann.

CHAPTER FOUR

Unconscious communication, psychoanalysis, and religious experience*

Marsha Aileen Hewitt

Introduction

> During psychoanalysis, the psychic contact between analyst and analysand is so intimate and the psychic processes which unfold themselves in that situation are so manifold that the analytic situation may well include all the conditions that facilitate the occurrence of occult phenomenon. These effects are probably connected with transference and seem to indicate the existence of an essential relationship between analytic intuition and the telepathic process.

That was stated in 1926 by Helene Deutsch, one of the early pioneers of psychoanalysis in a paper called "The Occult Processes Occurring during Psychoanalysis."

The telepathic process, that strange world full of charlatans and corner store clairvoyants—does that really exist in relation to the exquisite shared intersubjective space that can occur between analyst and patient? Can it really occur absent the hard fought-for emotional vulnerability that can

---

*This chapter includes abbreviated and edited sections from more extensive and detailed discussions in my book, *Legacies of the Occult: Psychoanalysis, Religion and Unconscious Communication.* Sheffield, UK: Equinox (2020). Reprinted with permission.

take years to unfold? And even if so, so what? Would it necessarily facilitate the healing analytic process? How would it deepen one's self-awareness allowing greater openness to new possibilities for growth?

As we will learn from Dr. Hewitt, unconscious communication or telepathy has a long, contentious, and indeed, secretive history in the development of psychoanalysis. Secretive because many of the early analytic pioneers lived in fear that the entire psychoanalytic enterprise would be associated with circus acts that parade themselves as mind readers. In fact, Freud, like Houdini, spent some time investigating such performers and either uncovered their trickery or alternatively reformulated their so-called discoveries as examples of familiar unconscious conflicts.

One reason analysts have a long history of cynicism concerning such seemingly magical, if not infantile powers, is that we so regularly find that supposed "thought transmission" can be better understood as reflecting the manifestations of intrapsychic repression. Nevertheless, there were a number of early analysts who would not entirely walk away from the subject. "Thought transference is where a verbal message gets transformed into a wave or ray of quite unknown nature and then on reception is reconverted into material terms." That was Freud (1915e, p. 194), quoted by his biographer and colleague Jones.

Further, in 1921, Freud wrote in a letter, "If I had to live my life over again I should devote myself to psychical research rather than psychoanalysis" (Jones, 1957, p. 419). Demonstrating how conflicted he was on the subject he later forgot that he wrote this letter and denied its existence. In fact, the letter was found eight years after he denied its existence.

These many years later we now find ourselves in a psychotherapy world where interrelational concepts are taken for granted. Terms like shared intersubjective space, unconscious attunement, the metabolizer of projective identifications, empathic contact, the analytic third—these are the underpinnings today of our everyday world. Do these represent our tolerance for greater clinical intimacy perhaps associated with stricter limits on physical interactions? Are these concepts related to the new neuro-biological findings of brain wave synchronization between speaker and listener? Are we more deeply approaching in a different language what Helene Deutsch characterized as "a central relationship between psycho-analytic intuition and the telepathic process"?

A few months ago my wife and I went to Africa on safari. In preparation for the trip, as is our inclination, we researched the sites we were to visit. One of the things I learned about was the relationship between the acacia tree and giraffes.

The foliage of the acacia tree is the favorite food of giraffes. Over the millennia they've been battling with each other for survival. Ages ago they were both much shorter than they are now. Evolutionarily, the acacia tree developed a strategy to defend itself against the giraffes who would otherwise consume them all. They grew taller. As we know, the giraffe selected out to do the same. Then the acacia tree developed thorns to protect its leaves. The giraffes in turn then developed long leathery tongues to work around the thorns. The acacia tree then developed the ability to secrete bitter tannins in its leaves when it is being attacked by giraffes. This dissuaded the giraffes from consuming too many of the leaves. The challenge for the tree was to secrete the indigestion-causing tannins quickly enough to thwart the giraffes. Researchers in the field discovered that when the leaves on tree A are being eaten the leaves on tree B fifty yards away would also secrete tannin though the roots were not connected. What was the nature of this "communication" between the trees?

The researchers discovered that a special breed of ants live on acacia trees. When the trees are being attacked by giraffes the ants secrete a substance that is carried by the wind to the ants on neighboring acacia trees who then alert the downwind tree that "The giraffes are coming!" That's communication on a literal level.

Let's move communication up a level of abstraction. Years ago when I started doing clinical work I observed what I thought was a strange phenomenon. On occasion while with a patient I had seemingly random thoughts go through my mind. Soon thereafter the individual I was with would say something often identical to what I had just been imagining. I found this quite strange. As an example, last week, I was sitting with a patient and an image of a young woman I know who's very eagerly looking for a job came to mind seemingly out of nowhere. Two minutes later the patient started talking about a person who came to her urgently seeking a job. She described feeling badly that she had not responded as promptly as she might have. We had long recognized her character trait of seeing neediness in others that in fact reflected her own, especially as she felt it between us. This incident allowed us another opportunity to rework this style of defense. But what to make of the fact that this manifest image was identical, almost word for word, to what had occurred in my mind a few moments before?

When I first started encountering these experiences, I was confused by them. I cautiously went to senior colleagues and related these events and asked them if this happened to them. They responded quite casually "Of course." I then asked how they understood what had happened. They responded somewhat formulaically by quoting Freud on unconscious communication—when one unconscious related to another's unconscious without going through consciousness. I was familiar with the quote but when I asked them what they actually thought that meant, they shrugged their shoulders.

I wondered whether, if this kind of communication can happen, as it seemingly can, might it also go the other way? My ability to tune into my patient's unconscious might give evidence of a patient's ability to tune into mine. Indeed there are a few courageous analytic writers who write about such things. We will hear more about this from Dr. Hewitt.

Let's move up to an even higher level of abstraction. The capacity to tune in to another's unconscious processes didn't begin with Freud. This ability has seemingly been with us throughout human history. It wasn't called telepathy a thousand years ago or unconscious communication five hundred years ago. What did they call it? Perhaps, just perhaps, this is what has been, and for some still is, called the divine. Maybe that's how this phenomenon has been understood throughout history. Maybe this relates to the notion that many people have, that there is God within us. Maybe the overlap of these domains explains the fact that when prior generations of analysts were asked about religion they answered, with solemnity, "Psychoanalysis is my religion."

Harvey Schwartz

* * *

Although Sigmund Freud was ambivalent about telepathy, he eventually conceded that it does exist because he experienced it in his clinical work. He regarded telepathy as a mental capacity that originates in the unconscious. Freud's earliest papers on the unconscious recognize that communication between patient and analyst occurs on the levels of both conscious and unconscious communication. Freud believed that the most important part of therapy occurs through what Ferenczi famously referred to as a dialogue of the unconscious where the unconscious of both analyst and patient drift, intermingle as they generate affective resonances between and around them. Freud encouraged analysts to cultivate this drift, counselling them to "turn [their] own unconscious like a receptive organ towards the transmitting unconscious of the patient" (1912e, p. 115). In a passage such as this, Freud is referring to the transfer of affects, where the analyst attempts to "pick up" the patient's feelings which remain hidden to consciousness. It is the job of the analyst to interpret the patient's unconscious feelings and conflicts and translate them into language that will hopefully promote deeper self-understanding and symptom relief. Over time, unconscious communication included more than the affect transfer of the patient's inchoate feeling states. In some clinical situations, Freud's patients "knew" things about him they could not have discovered by conventional communicative means.

Telepathic knowing, which Freud also described as "thought-transference" or "unconscious communication" often occurs in dreams. However, Freud insisted that there is no such thing as a "telepathic dream" (1933a-1). Rather, there are dreams that *may contain* telepathic elements, fragments of experience or knowledge from the waking states of the day's residues that only become clear during a dream. What we consciously know is not always identical to what we may perceive at the edges of consciousness that may later manifest in a dream. Since Freud, a growing number of psychoanalysts have been writing about telepathic experiences with patients, most often in the form of a dream a patient has that contains details about the analyst's private life. Psychoanalysts have begun to overcome their understandable anxiety about openly discussing such experiences. Part of the reason for this has to do with changing understandings of the nature of intersubjectivity, and an increasing acknowledgment that the psychological borders demarcating self and other may not be as clear as once assumed. As I explain below, there is a growing psychoanalytic literature that views the borders of individual subjectivity as permeable and fluid. Where the self ends and the other begins cannot be always clearly established. When the minds of the patient and the analyst "meet" in dreams, things can become quite unsettling.

The dream[1]

One Monday morning, Kate, who had been in a four times weekly analysis for several years, recounted a dream she had about her analyst during the previous weekend:

> You were in a large house, like a Thirties-style mansion or maybe a hotel, and it was on the beach, by an ocean, I think. The house had several large rooms and you were always with large groups of people, talking to them, drinking something, or listening to others. It was a really beautiful place, this huge mansion-type house, on a beach at the edge of a large sea or ocean. I think maybe it had a pool as well, I can't remember. You seemed to be having a good time.

On the weekend in question the analyst had attended a conference at a lavish, Art Deco-style hotel in southern California that had an outdoor pool overlooking the beach and ocean beyond. This particular conference had no concurrent panels, but was organized around consecutive plenary sessions. This meant the analyst was always with large groups of people in the hotel ballroom where the speakers presented. In the breaks between papers the conference participants gathered for coffee and continued conversation. It was a stimulating conference and a very pleasant weekend for the analyst. At no time prior to the weekend had the analyst told Kate anything of her whereabouts or even that she would be out of town. It was highly unlikely that Kate could have had any knowledge about the conference or her analyst's plans to attend it. No sessions had been missed, no times had been rearranged. As Kate described her dream, the analyst experienced a physical shock of uncanniness: *Her patient had dreamed her weekend, in astonishing detail.* What was going on here?

In the early years of analytic work, Kate was invariably anxious around breaks, particularly those involving missed sessions. She said she was frightened that she would never see her therapist again. It was difficult for Kate to hold her therapist in her mind and feel an ongoing internal connection with her. Kate often needed concrete demonstrations of care not only from her therapist, but also from others. She could only feel reassurance of her boyfriend's love in moments of physical intimacy with him. When he travelled for work, she became very anxious that he forgot about her, or would meet someone else. For her, "out of sight" meant literally "out of mind."

She often worried that her analyst might one day just "disappear." On a conscious level, Kate worried something "bad" might happen to her analyst, especially during vacation breaks. However, unconsciously she was terrified that her analyst would forget *her*. Sometimes her therapist gave her a small object from the office to hold while she was on vacation. Concrete objects belonging to the therapist helped Kate to *hold onto* their relationship, which helped her to *hold onto* her (experience of) self. Without a tangible, concrete connection with another person, Kate's existential sense of "ontological security" (Laing, 1959, p. 39) was threatened. Sometimes the analyst gave her a phone number where she could be reached if necessary, although Kate never called while her analyst was away. She just needed to know that she *could*, and having the number written down in her therapist's handwriting had a calming effect on her. These symbolic linking gestures helped Kate contain her anxiety around planned separations. This arrangement went on for the first few years of the analysis, and seemed to work well. When the analyst returned, Kate was able to reflect upon her feelings and fantasies in ways that showed progress in her ability to tolerate separations.

As such negotiated arrangements were made only for extended vacation periods and not for typical weekend breaks, the analyst saw no reason to tell Kate that she would be out of town over the weekend in question. As far as Kate knew, this would be a weekend break like any other. However, the "dumbfounding precision" (Eshel, 2006, p. 1619) of her uncannily accurate dream showed that Kate knew a great deal about her analyst. From a psychoanalytic perspective, Kate's dream dramatically revealed that important therapeutic progress had been quietly taking place between them. The analyst was aware that Kate had been developing an increasingly robust capacity to remain mentally connected to her during periods of physical separation, and was heartened by this development. What the analyst did not know, could not have known, was that Kate was able to maintain contact with her in unsettling ways. Her dream was an eerie demonstration that she could find her therapist if her need to was powerful enough.

Dreams such as Kate's are neither new nor particularly rare in the psychoanalytic literature. To this day, no one knows exactly how telepathic communication works. Freud certainly didn't, but he believed that one day science would be able to explain it. He wondered if telepathy, or unconscious communication was a vestige from primordial times when language had not yet been developed. He was also adamant that dreams are not telepathic, even if telepathic communication seems to occur sometimes in them (1933a.i). In the cases of telepathic dreaming or apparently tele-pathically acquired knowledge on the part of a patient, Freud would focus on the relationship between the parties involved. He was not particularly interested in trying to explain the accuracy of detail of such dreams. How-ever, since his time, psychoanalysts are becoming increasingly interested in how telepathy might work as well as acknowledging the importance of the relationships involved. These dreams challenge psychoanalysis at the very least to question and transform its usual presuppositions about the nature *and* potentialities of human consciousness, and the permeability of psychic boundaries. It is increasingly acknowledged within psychoanaly-sis that "telepathic" dreams are most commonly associated with trauma-based pathology (Schore, 2012, p. 177). Kate's dream was a powerful psychic remnant of a traumatic past generally characterized by sustained dread of abandonment which was reignited by her unconscious knowledge not only of her therapist's *impending* absence, but of an emotional unconscious psy-chological "absence" or distraction in her caused by her excited anticipation about the conference.

In the weeks preceding her dream, Kate was experiencing a "state of intense positive dependent transference" (Balint, 1955, p. 32). Her "tele-pathic" dream was a "desperate means of communication" whereby she struggled to (re)gain the analyst's "full attention" (p. 32). In her dream Kate found a way to remain connected to her analyst across a vast geographical distance. By "joining" the analyst through her dream, Kate demonstrated her newly acquired capacity to regulate the painful anxiety of separation by *creating* the analyst in her mind. Kate's dream poignantly and powerfully communicated her feelings of being marginalized and displaced. Vitally important psychic changes had been taking place both *within* Kate and *within the analytic relationship* that remained outside the awareness of them both. Kate found an elegant and, for the analyst, disturbing "telepathic" way to communicate this as yet unformulated awareness through her newly acquired capacity to dream her into the world of another. Whether her dream was a product of clairvoyant power on Kate's part or any other form of "super human" phenomenon is impossible to establish, and beyond the scope of psychoanalytic knowledge. My focus here is on the *clinically* impor-tant question of how to think *psychoanalytically* about Kate's dream. The astounding accuracy of detail in the dream, while not insignificant, must for now remain a mystery. I agree with Balint that "In order to study para-psychological phenomena profitably we should not concentrate on either the subject's receptive powers or the healer's or agent's influencing powers, but on the powers *inherent in their mutual relation*" (p. 35, emphasis added).

For Balint, the putative uncanny experiences increasingly reported by clinicians (Bass, 2001; Eisold, 2002; Farrell, 1983; Jacobs, 2001; Marcus, 1997; Mayer, 2001, 2008) are best approached psychoanalytically. His view coincides with Freud's approach which holds that such experiences seem to occur most often in dream or other altered mental states and almost always in contexts of intense, affectively charged relationships. Considered from Freud's perspective, Kate's unconscious awareness of her analyst's distracted state remained unformulated until it could be made available to her in her dream. Kate's dream was precipitated by a different kind of weekend break that symbolized the temporarily attenuated clinical intimacy which in turn aroused the accumulated trauma of childhood abandonment. This interpretation recalls Freud's (1925i) view that "Telepathic messages received in the course of the day may only be dealt with during a dream of the following night" (p. 138). The "telepathic" exchange between Kate and her analyst was provoked by her sense of a "distance" between them. In her dream, Kate was able to establish a kind of "telepathic" bridge linking the multiple layers of distance that were coming between her and the analyst.

Contemporary psychoanalysis argues with increasing openness that putative "telepathic" (*tele* = distance, *pathos* = feeling, suffering) experience is an intrinsic, if not central part, of unconscious communication. Psychoanalytic theories of the unconscious, the nature of transference/ countertransference, projective identification, and dream analysis can provide important resources for efforts to address this phenomenon. Freud's steadfast opposition to *supernatural* explanations of uncanny human experiences (which for him belonged to religion and faith) did not prevent him from recognizing and accepting that minds are capable of communicating outside or beyond the conventional modalities of language and physical cues. For Freud, unconscious communication between analyst and patient was a key component of therapeutic action.

Metaphorically drawing upon the new teletechnologies of his day, Freud (1912e) counseled that the analyst "must turn his own unconscious like a receptive organ towards the transmitting unconscious of the patient. He must adjust himself to the patient as a telephone receiver is adjusted to the transmitting microphone" (pp. 115–116). The minds of both the analyst and patient meet through powerful, multivalent, and affective communicational avenues that are generated by and envelop them both. Each "feels" the other. For Freud (1925i) "thought-transference" occurs as "an idea emerges from the unconscious" as it "passes over from 'primary process' to the 'secondary process'" mentation (p. 138). Most importantly, the presence of intense relational affects/emotions are central to shared "telepathic" communicative experience.

Understandably, most psychoanalysts are at a loss to explain the specific details associated with uncanny experiences. While analysts "seldom understand how we intuit what we know" (Eisold, 2002, p. 516), some counsel focusing on "what actually occurs without worrying about how it [can] be explained" (p. 517). This is the goal of therapeutic action that should take precedence over efforts to explain the technology of telepathy. As Helene Deutsch (1926) commented with regard to her own clinical experience of unconscious communication, they "confirm that 'occult' powers are to be sought in the depth of psychic life" (p. 146). Psychoanalysis is inevitably a multidisciplinary enterprise that draws on both the humanities and the sciences. As psychoanalysis wonders more explicitly about unconscious communication, it opens itself to dialogue with other disciplines such as religion. However, psychoanalysis must maintain its central focus on the *psychoanalytic* meaning of specific therapeutic relationships. As clinicians, we must not lose sight of the fact that therapeutic action takes place *within* the intense emotional connectedness of the analytic relationship created *between* the analytic partners who are not as separately distinct as they perceive (or would prefer) themselves to be. Sometimes, weird things happen.

Permeable minds: Hans Loewald

Hans Loewald's theory of *interpenetrating psyches* contributes to our thinking *psychoanalytically* about the nature of unconscious communication and how it occurs. It also brings a spiritual or religious quality to it. Loewald frames the concept of infant/mother connectivity in terms of a shared psychic or "love" matrix that is generated by them and envelops them both (2000, pp. 10–12, 553–554). Mother and infant exist together in mutual empathic communication that is punctuated by fusion states *and* a gradually developing awareness of difference. The boundaries between self and other are fluid and permeable in early infancy. This view draws upon Freud's (1933a.ii) later theory of mind where ego and superego *differentiation* emerges or shades out of their common source, the id. A reasonably healthy mother is able to open her mind to receive and read the mind of her infant.

In healthy enough environments, the infantile sense of self-in-and-with-other constitutes the unconscious source of potential artistic and intellectual creativity, including mystical or spiritual experiences of unity or oneness with the world experienced in adulthood. Mystical states of unity with all reality, the *unio mystica*, that occurs in adulthood draws upon unconscious memory traces of infantile fusion states with the mother. Loewald's idea of the psychic matrix is the originary source, rooted in real experience, of what later may be revived in experiences that individuals deem to be mystical or spiritual.

For Loewald, the conscious and unconscious dimensions of the psyche become capable of fostering and strengthening interconnected linkages through a developmental process of *differentiation*. These internal connections are vulnerable to a variety of distortions due to environmental trauma and/or neglect with the result that the individual experiences aspects of his or her mind as terrifyingly alien or "other." The feeling of being "possessed" by spirits is an example of this. In thinking about oneself, one cannot help but objectify the self in order to think about it. In more optimal environmental conditions, psychic linkages between mental states are established and cultivated; the unconscious provides a (re)source of vitality and creative energy that enlivens conscious awareness and action. One is able to integrate a variety of emotional states within the larger personality, and claim them as one's own. The interpenetrability or linking of mental states *within* the mind facilitates possibilities for connections between or with other minds or transcendent realities. Such experiences can be exhilarating or terrifying, and sometimes both. In altered or hypnoid states of consciousness, the individual may feel that his mind has been "invaded" or "taken over" by another entity, as can occur in varying degrees of dissociation and, in extreme cases, psychosis. The more positive, other side of this experience is a feeling of being filled with the Holy Spirit, or a sense of a temporary merger with the universe. Both experiences, negative and positive, are most often understood as types of spiritual states of communion with transcendent dimensions.

Freud describes the internal state of the neonate as expanding outward in a movement of libidinal energy that gathers in elements of the loved objects/others that become internalized through identifications that deepen and differentiate the infant's developing mental states. From Loewald's point of view, this suggests that in earliest infancy, the sense of self and sense of external reality comprise merger or fusion states within the maternal/infant psychic matrix. In other words, the infant does not confront reality "out there" as separate, but reality exists "in here." What we call "in here" and "out there" is the result of a developmental process of differentiation and integration that is part of the trajectory of Eros as it seeks the forging of relationships with the world. Consideration of the notion of the "oceanic feeling" that Freud (1930a) addressed in response to Romain Rolland, is pertinent here. Rolland believed that the *unio mystica*, or feeling of "eternity" and oneness constituted the origin of religion, rather than the unconscious need for paternal protection and safety that Freud postulated in *The Future of an Illusion* (1927c).

Although Freud confesses that he has never personally experienced the oceanic feeling, he nonetheless cannot accept that "the primary nature of such a feeling" is the source of religious experience and belief (1930a, p. 65). Nevertheless, Freud takes Rolland's thesis that the oceanic feeling is the source of religion seriously as he attempts to conceptualize and explain it psychoanalytically.[2] Drawing upon his earlier idea of "primary narcissism" (1914c), Freud theorizes that in very early infancy, the child cannot "distinguish his ego from the external world as the source of the sensations flowing in upon him" (1930a, p. 67). The developing child only gradually acquires self-awareness and the distinctions between self and other in response to "various promptings" from the external world (p. 67). In adulthood, memory traces of this stage of development may become activated for a variety of reasons in mystical or spiritual experiences that Rolland described as eternal connectedness with the universe. As Loewald (2000) later observed, largely in agreement with Freud's speculation, this "primordial type of experience is not unique to the mother–infant matrix. It, or its *direct derivatives*, are encountered in various forms in adult experience" (p. 554).

For both Freud and Loewald, the mind initially is a formless unity that becomes increasingly differentiated and complex in its ongoing interactions with the world. What is particularly relevant to the notion of unconscious communication or telepathy is Loewald's idea that there is no "primordial individual self or individual instinctive core but [rather] a wider 'subjectivity' that includes the creative-destructive powers of the parental couple" (2000, p. 516, italics added). This idea extends to include the notion that nature is conscious, so that "individual mentation" is "but one instance or manifestation of *natura naturans*, of nature's 'subjectivity'" (p. 516). Here Loewald goes beyond Freud as he broaches the idea of panpsychism in which a wider, cosmic consciousness flows through all of nature as a connecting current of interpenetrating, individual subjectivities. Although Loewald does not address the idea of telepathy, the panpsychic implications of his thought very much supports it.

James Grotstein: The mystical truth of psychoanalysis[3]

The late Kleinian analyst James Grotstein elaborates upon the mystical nature of subjectivity and the interpenetrability of individual and cosmic minds in a far more explicitly religious fashion than Loewald. In his *Who Is the Dreamer Who Dreams the Dream?* (2000), Grotstein attempts to reformulate Freud's theory of dreams in spiritual, mystical terms. For Grotstein, the dream is a mystical portal through which the "numinous origins" of "ultimate mystery," "Absolute Truth," or "Ultimate and Infinite Reality" (2009, pp. 746, 749) can be experienced. At their deepest levels, dreams act as an interface between cosmic spirit and its individualized presence as instantiated in the dreamer's mind. Grotstein's "Ultimate and Infinite Reality" heavily elaborates Wilfred Bion's (1897–1979) enigmatic notion of "O", a concept derived from religions and neo-Platonic philosophy. With Grotstein in particular, clinical work is a form of spiritual practice, a "sacred analytic passion play" (Grotstein, 2000, p. 237) through which the analyst-priest (p. 244) absorbs the patient's pain (p. 233). Bion writes that he

> ... use(s) the sign O to denote that which is the ultimate reality represented by terms such as ultimate reality, absolute truth, the godhead, the infinite, the thing-in-itself. O ... can "become", but it cannot be "known". It is darkness and formlessness ... its presence can be recognized and felt ... The religious mystics have probably approximated most closely to expression of experience of it. Its existence is as essential to science as to religion. (1970, pp. 26, 30)

From a Bionian perspective, psychoanalytic work may reveal "glimpses of O, the preexisting unity that is ultimate reality" (White, 2011, p. 233). "O," whose existence is "conjectured phenomenologically," (Bion, 1970, p. 26) is the "origin" or the "One" (White, 2011, p. 226), "the generator of the Forms, or what Bion terms pre-conceptions" (ibid.). Individual learning is a process of *recollection* of an original oneness that was split and fragmented in "the catastrophic divisions of birth" and later life traumas (ibid.). In Grotstein's view, "the unconscious capacity for prescience and premonition" found in dreams suggests that "one aspect of the self seems to be superior in knowl-edge to our more ordinary self" (Grotstein, 2000, p. xxviii) because of the "mystical," "preternatural," or "numinous" nature of the unconscious. He attempts to revise Freud's idea of the unconscious in terms of a divine essence whose spiritual nature is "like a god" that dwells within the "sacred architecture of the psyche" (p. xxiii). Here Grotstein clearly interprets Bion's "O" as a "cosmic consciousness" (2000, p. 284) that both congeals in and flows through individual minds. This mystical reality can be occasionally glimpsed in dreams. Dreams function as a "contact-barrier" that organizes, protects, and mediates "the impingements of 'O'" (2009, p. 734) which may be chaotic and dangerously overwhelming to the dreamer. Dreaming acts as a "filter for unmentalized infinite emotional Truth" (p. 734), or "sensory overload" (p. 738) of "O." Dreaming "perceives, anticipates, and formats oncoming premonitory experiences" (p. 739). Dreams are "memoir[s] of the future," a listening-in on the secret conversations of the gods (2000, pp. 28–29). The dreamer who dreams the dream is the "elusive, ineffable subject within us" who "lurks on the other side" of the deepest recesses of the dream (2000, p. 1).

Freud and mysticism?

There is a long-standing assumption in the history of psychoanalysis that Freud's theories contain hidden mystical dimensions that resonate strongly with esoteric traditions such as Jewish mysticism and Kabbalah (Bakan, 1958; Roback, 1929). Grotstein in some ways shares this view while also pointing out "Freud's own 'religion' of 'science,' logical positivism" (2004, p. 82). Nonetheless, Grotstein tries to argue that a hidden religiosity lies within "Freud's concept of the unconscious [which can] be understood as the closest to the idea of God that man can possibly contemplate and that he has contemplated this deity as a heavenly projective identification" (2004, p. 91). He makes a futile effort to show that Freud was a closet mystic who could not allow himself to connect with his own inherent spirituality. Grotstein thinks that Freud's excessive focus on "science" blinded him to the mystical nature of the unconscious. Freud, however, did not agree that his view of the uncon-scious was compatible with spiritual or religious interpretation: "I think I am farthest from being a mystic" (in Wulff, 1991, p. 261). Freud's notion of the unconscious is different than Grotstein's description of the unconscious as a "mystical, preternatural, numinous second self" (2000, p. xvi). Although unacknowledged, not only by both Bion and Grotstein, it is important to point out that the religious psychology of William James and his friend and colleague, the psychic researcher, psychological theorist, and Cambridge classicist Frederic Myers (1843–1901) resonates strongly in the mystical psychoanalysis represented by Bion and especially Grotstein.

F. W. H. Myers, forerunner of contemporary psychoanalysis and spirituality

Frederic W. H. Myers was familiar with Freud's and Breuer's work on hysteria, which he introduced to the English-speaking world toward the end of the nineteenth century. Myers also believed that consciousness does not represent the major portion of mental life. His view of the unconscious as a system of dissociated states or multiple consciousnesses differed from Freud's theory of repression and conflict. Myers rejected the term unconscious in favor of the subconscious, or subliminal self, that existed below the threshold of ordinary consciousness. This hidden psychic dimension of the self was for him the source of "super normal" capacities revealed in dreams, hallucinations, dissociated states, clairvoyance, telepathy, flashes of unusual genius, and authentic mediumistic communication with the spirits of the dead. Exploration of the subliminal self, or subconscious in hypnoid states led not only to super normal abilities, but also to transcendent realms of reality beyond the individual. The parallels with Grotstein are striking, although Grotstein never mentions Myers in his work.

The cornerstone of Myers' psychology was his belief in the survival of the human personality after bodily death. Myers argued that the individual *sub*conscious or "subliminal self" (1961, pp. 26–27, 205–206) originates in a universal, cosmic mind within which it is reabsorbed after death. It cannot be overemphasized that Myers' theory of a "subliminal self" is radically different from what Freud understood as the unconscious. Myers' mystical psychology conceived of a *subliminal* consciousness, deriving from a wider, cosmic mind-at-large, that contained super normal potentials for forms of extraordinary knowing such as telepathy, clairvoyance, and communication with discarnate spirits. These occult or hidden super normal powers that lay dormant in human beings may be released in uprushes of subliminal energies into the supraliminal or conscious self. For Myers' close friend and colleague, the American psychologist, philosopher, and psychic researcher William James, the subliminal self is "the fountain-head of much that feeds our religion" (in Wulff, 1991, p. 489). The sacred, in the view of Myers and James, was an element in the structure of the mind that represented an energy or power of human potential that is part of our evolutionary progression.

In sharp contrast to Myers and James, Freud's acknowledgment of the reality of thought-transference or telepathy can in no way be understood as providing "evidence of man's survival of death" or the existence of super normal powers. The Freudian unconscious has nothing to do with a "subliminal faculty" that persists after organic death, nor does it have a cosmic genesis. While neither Freud nor Myers understood how thought-transference actually takes place, and while both located it outside of conscious awareness, their respective notions of an unconscious (Freud) and a subliminal self (Myers) represents a clear difference between them. Freud's view that the unconscious of the analyst is an affective medium that connects with the unconscious of his patient did not lead him to conclude, as Myers did, that there is an "essential unity of the human spirit and the universe" (in Kripal, 2007, p. 409). Grotstein, who stands in the tradition of mystical psychology represented by Myers, would agree that all material and human existence originates in the cosmic mind.

Freud accepted that thought-transference was a natural phenomenon that sometimes occurs in the course of clinical work (Hewitt, 2014). He tried, perhaps unsuccessfully, to establish strong demarcations between telepathy as a purely psychological, not religious phenomenon. The fact that the unconscious is "mysterious" (Freud, 1941d, p. 180) in no way meant that it was *mystical*. These terms are not synonymous. Freud insisted that telepathy was a capacity of unconscious mentation that remained unexplained by science and nothing more than that. However, the mystical, religious appeal of unconscious communication, or telepathy, was too powerful for psychoanalysis after Freud to resist. The metaphysical psychology of Frederic Myers and his close friend, colleague, and fellow psychical researcher William James continues to exert a powerful and enduring influence on contemporary psychoanalysis. Increasingly, contemporary psychoanalysis describes instances of unconscious communication in clinical contexts as ineffable, "chimeric" (Eshel, 2012) moments of analyst/patient interconnectedness that, while defying ordinary forms of discursive expression and scientific explanation, are transmuting and transforming for *both* parties. As we saw with Kate's dream, apparent telepathic communications can occur both within the analytic hour or outside it. They can extend beyond the consulting room as unconscious knowledge that each individual has about the other but which remains unformulated and thus unavailable to consciousness until it is ready to break through in a "telepathic," or unconscious communication, such as a dream.

For Frederic Myers, telepathy provided powerful evidence for the existence of super normal mental powers that resonate with later quantum theories of nonlocality, or entanglement. This refers to experiments with particles separated across vast distances, where measuring activity applied to one of the particles will produce identical results in the other. Another related notion that psychoanalysis takes from quantum physics concerns the interconnected nature of the observer and the observed. Many analysts invoke these ideas in their efforts to explain how unconscious communication occurs as a flow of psychic energies between permeable minds. Some contemporary analysts find powerful support in these ideas for their theories of the unbounded, "irreducible" nature of individual minds (Mayer, 2008). Although a detailed discussion of psychoanalysis and the paranormal is beyond the scope of this essay,[4] it should be noted that some analytic writers such as Elizabeth Lloyd Mayer extend psychoanalysis into the field of parapsychology as they seek to explain a wide range of psychic phenomena that include remote viewing, precognition, and divination. These approaches continue in the nineteenth-century tradition of Frederic Myers, whose psychological theories were inextricably entwined with his investigations in psychical research. The notion of the deep interconnectedness of all reality is reflected both in his theory of a unitary cosmic mind that instantiates in individual personalities and in contemporary psychoanalysis that relies on quantum ideas to validate its metaphysical, mystical insights.

Although almost entirely unacknowledged, it is Myers and James, not Freud, who are the intellectual ancestors of what may be reasonably called mystical psychoanalysis. The turn away from the Freudian unconscious in favor of a Myersian/Jamesian subconscious allows spiritually oriented analysts such as James Grotstein to declare that "Psychoanalysis is more mystical, spiritual and religious than its followers realize, and religion, especially spirituality, is more psychoanalytic than its followers realize" (2004, p. 93). As one sympathetic commentator observes, Grotstein has written the "gnostic gospel of depth psychology" (Gordon, 2004, p. 18). The intersection of Grotstein's gnostic psychoanalytic vision represents a contemporary, thoroughly *modern* psychoanalysis resurrected and refashioned out of its nineteenth-century roots in the *modern* occult psychology of

Frederic Myers. If we regard Freud's theory of the unconscious as a branch on the evolutionary tree of modern psychology, it may not survive the growing developments of a visionary and mystical psychoanalysis whose goal is to lead the individual on an inward path to the gnosis of his or her own inner sacred psychic architecture. From this perspective, Freud is the discarded "other" of psychoanalysis.

Notes

1. See my *Legacies of the Occult* (2020) for a more detailed and extended discussion of Kate's dream and various psychoanalytic interpretations of it.
2. See my *Freud on Religion* (2014, pp. 48–50), and *Legacies of the Occult* (in press, 2020) for a more detailed contextual and theoretical analysis of Freud's exchanges with Rolland.
3. This section is a highly abbreviated version of a lengthier and more detailed discussion of the mystical psychoanalysis of Grotstein and Bion in my *Legacies of the Occult* (in press, 2020).
4. See chapter 4 in my *Legacies of the Occult* for a full discussion of psychoanalysis and its use of ideas from quantum theory, and what I call "parapsychoanalysis."

References

Bakan, D. (1958). *Sigmund Freud and the Jewish Mystical Tradition.* Princeton, NJ: Van Nostrand.

Balint, M. (1955). Notes on parapsychology and parapsychological healing. *International Journal of Psychoanalysis, 36*: 31–35.

Bass, A. (2001). It takes one to know one; or, whose unconscious is it anyway? *Psychoanalytic Dialogues, 11*: 683–702.

Bion, W. R. (1970). *Attention and Interpretation.* London: Karnac.

Deutsch, H. (1926). Occult processes occurring during psychoanalysis. In: G. Devereux (Ed.), *Psychoanalysis and the Occult* (pp. 133–146). New York: International Universities Press, 1953.

Eisold, K. (2002). Jung, Jungians, and psychoanalysis. *Psychoanalytic Psychology, 19*: 501–524.

Eshel, O. (2006). Where are you, my beloved?: On absence, loss, and the enigma of telepathic dreams. *International Journal of Psychoanalysis, 87*: 1603–1627.

Eshel, O. (2012). A beam of "chimeric" darkness: Presence, interconnectedness, and transformation in the psychoanalytic treatment of a patient convicted of sex offenses. *Psychoanalytic Review, 99*: 149–178.

Farrell, D. (1983). Freud's "thought-transference," repression, and the future of psychoanalysis. *International Journal of Psychoanalysis, 64*: 71–81.

Freud, S. (1912e). Recommendations to physicians practising psycho-analysis. *S. E., 12*: 111–120. London: Hogarth.

Freud, S. (1914c). On narcissism: an introduction. *S. E., 14*: 211–238. London: Hogarth.

Freud, S. (1915e). The unconscious. *S. E., 14*: 166–215. London: Hogarth.

Freud, S. (1925i). Some additional notes on dream-interpretation as a whole. *S. E., 19*: 127–138. London: Hogarth.

Freud, S. (1927c). *The Future of an Illusion. S. E., 21*: 5–56. London: Hogarth.

Freud, S. (1930a). *Civilization and Its Discontents. S. E., 21*: 59–145. London: Hogarth.

Freud, S. (1933a.i). Dreams and occultism. In: *New Introductory Lectures on Psycho-Analysis. S. E., 22*: 31–56. London: Hogarth.

Freud, S. (1933a.ii). The dissection of the psychical personality. In: *New Introductory Lectures on Psycho-Analysis. S. E., 22*: 57–80. London: Hogarth.

Freud, S. (1941d). Psycho-analysis and telepathy. *S. E., 18*: 177–193. London: Hogarth.

Gordon, K. (2004). The tiger's stripe: Some thoughts on psychoanalysis, gnosis, and the experience of wonderment. *Contemporary Psychoanalysis, 40*: 5–45.

Grotstein, J. S. (2000). *Who Is the Dreamer Who Dreams the Dream?: A Study of Psychic Presences*. Hillsdale, NJ: Analytic Press.

Grotstein, J. S. (2004). Spirituality, religion, politics, history, apocalypse and transcendence: An essay on a psychoanalytically and religiously forbidden subject. *International Journal of Applied Psychoanalytic Studies, 1*: 82–95.

Grotstein, J. S. (2009). Dreaming as a "curtain of illusion": Revisiting the "royal road" with Bion as our guide. *International Journal of Psychoanalysis, 90*: 733–752.

Hewitt, M. A. (2014). *Freud on Religion*. Durham, UK: Acumen.

Hewitt, M. A. (2020). *Legacies of the Occult: Psychoanalysis, Religion and Unconscious Communication*. Sheffield, UK: Equinox.

Jacobs, T. J. (2001). On unconscious communications and covert enactments: Some reflections on their role in the analytic situation. *Psychoanalytic Inquiry, 21*: 4–23.

Jones, E. (1957). *Sigmund Freud: Life and Work, vol. 3, The Last Phase 1919–1939*. London: Hogarth.

Kripal, J. J. (2007). *Esalen: America and the Religion of No Religion*. Chicago, IL: University of Chicago Press.

Laing, R. D. (1959). *The Divided Self: An Existential Study in Sanity and Madness*. London: Penguin, 1965.

Lazar, S. G. (2001). Knowing, influencing, and healing: Paranormal phenomena and implications of psychoanalysis and psychotherapy. *Psychoanalytic Inquiry, 21*: 113–131.

Loewald, H. (2000). *The Essential Loewald: Collected Papers and Monographs.* Hagerstown, MD: University Publishing Group.

Marcus, D. M. (1997). On knowing what one knows. *Psychoanalytic Quarterly, 66*(2): 219–241.

Mayer, E. L. (2001). On "Telepathic Dreams?": An unpublished paper by Robert J. Stoller (1973). *Journal of the American Psychoanalytic Association, 49*: 635–652.

Mayer, E. L. (2008). *Extraordinary Knowing: Science, Skepticism, and the Inexplicable Powers of the Human Mind.* New York: Bantam.

Myers, F. W. H. (1961). *Human Personality and Its Survival of Bodily Death.* S. Smith (Ed.). Mineola, NY: Dover, 2005.

Roback, A. A. (1929). *Jewish Influence in Modern Thought.* Cambridge, MA: Sci-Art Publishers.

Schore, A. N. (2012). *The Science of the Art of Psychotherapy.* New York: W. W. Norton.

White, R. S. (2011). Bion and mysticism: The Western tradition. *American Imago, 68*(2): 213–240.

Wulff, D. M. (1991). *Psychology of Religion: Classic and Contemporary Views.* New York: John Wiley & Sons.

CHAPTER FIVE

Psychoanalysis in Israel: trauma, anti-Semitism, and victimization

Eran Rolnik

Introduction

Terroir. "*Terroir*" is a French term that refers to the totality of the environmental factors that impact the expression of a plant's essence. It is most often used in reference to the growing of grapes and the character of the resulting wine. Many factors influence the *terroir* of grapes—the soil composition, the angle of the sun, the air currents, the proximity to water, to name but a few. The subtle and at times dramatic differences in *terroir* account for the fact that the same grapes grown in Oregon, Burgundy, and New Zealand will express themselves quite differently in the wines produced in each region. These differing environmental contexts similarly play a role in the development of a psychoanalyst. The cultural zeitgeist in Vienna, Jerusalem, and Philadelphia differ as much as the aforementioned pinot noir growing regions.

To extend this metaphor a bit—it has long been considered that the soil characteristics in these vinicultural regions contribute essential and unique elements to their wines. Basalt and sandstone in the Willamette Valley, for example, are said to contribute a minerality to its wine. The quartz and mica schists that make up the soil of the Central Otago region in New Zealand are said to yield the unique earthiness of its wines, and so on.

There are both similarities and differences in the wines that emerge from each region.

Likewise, the cultural soil and time period of *fin de siècle* Vienna has been well studied and appreciated. It was a time of transition and social upheaval. It was also the time of Dreyfus. Peter Gay (1984) characterized it as the period when "the age of Victoria merged into the age of Freud." There was a collision of tensions born from the idealization of socialism, the constant immigration of Eastern European Jews (it was called the "Jewish invasion"), anti-Semitism, and German–Czech antagonisms throughout the region. Mark Twain visited during this period and noted that in some towns the Germans rioted and in other towns the Czechs rioted "and in all cases the Jew had to roast, no matter which side he was on" (1899, p. 249). We could in our own twenty-first century use a Mark Twain to take note of the anti-Semitisms today from both the right and the left. This Viennese setting was also the birthplace of early Zionism. In fact for two years Theodore Herzl lived down the street from Freud though they never met. Herzl's son though later consulted Freud as a patient (Skibell, 2002).

America was recognized as having a quite different soil for the growth of its version of psychoanalysis. While vast in its differing climates from coast to coast the States was initially disparaged as a suitable vineyard for this delicate fruit. Freud who visited once in 1909 had few good things to say about what he saw as the American temperament. He felt that our tendencies toward prudishness along with our materialistic focus would not offer rich earth for the open-minded thoughtfulness essential for the study of psychoanalysis. He saw America as representing New World ready-made cheerfulness in place of Old World substantive exploration. Indeed, he wrote to Ferenczi on January 10, 1909, "Once the Americans realize the sexual basis of our ideas, we'll be up shit creek" (Brabant, Falzeder, & Giampieri-Deutsch, 1993, p. 33). To add a dramatic flourish to this sentiment, he borrowed imagery from an early 1800s German playwright William Grabb: "America and psychoanalysis are as ill-adapted for one another that it is 'as though a raven were to put on a white shirt'" (Wittels, 1924, p. 130). He felt that the American's inclination to sensationalize nuances would contribute to a basic misunderstanding of the subtleties of an analyzed life. Some locate this characteristic to this day in American-made wines.

In this chapter we are to learn about the *terroir* of Israel as it expresses itself in its own unique psychoanalysis. Is there something particular in

Israel's historical and cultural context that makes for its own version of psychoanalysis? How do the continuous challenges to its existential legitimacy, not to mention constant external threats of annihilation, impact the delicate process of quiet mutual introspection? How does the intense communalism of this small nation impact the individual focus of a one, perhaps two, person psychotherapy? What is the impact of Israeli multiculturalism on its psychoanalysis which flourishes as nowhere else in the world?

These structural differences in cultural soils do exist and do influence much in our lives, vinous and psychotherapeutic. And yet. There is recent research that leads us to recognize an essential similarity among these differences. For example, it has been newly discovered that different soil compositions do not in and of themselves have the previously assumed impact on wine characteristics (Maltman, 2018). After all, slate, limestone, and quartz do not themselves insinuate flavors into growing grapes. Their contribution is now being understood as based on the microbiome that they encourage and the water drainage that they permit. That is, it appears that differing soil types needn't in and of themselves yield different flavor profiles just as different historical contexts needn't determine psychoanalytic practices and understanding. There is an expressed essence that is common to well-made wines. There is also an essence common to the experience of psychoanalysis. Perhaps this is related to the same essence that Freud alluded to in his oft quoted statement that even without an allegiance to religious rituals he nevertheless felt that in his "essence" he is a Jew (Preface to the Hebrew edition of *Totem and Taboo*, 1912–13).

Psychoanalysis can speak to us all despite our differences. In common we humans were all vulnerable children with more or less similarly developing brains subject to the vagaries of our real and perceived environments. We all depended on flawed caregivers, relied on our young fragile imaginations, and were driven to engage as best we could with the variously frustrating and satisfying world around us.

Psychoanalysis, imperfect but vital, in New Zealand and Vienna, in Jerusalem and Oregon, was created to liberate for all of us the essence of our internal nature to allow for the truest harvest of our personal bounty.

Harvey Schwartz

* * *

Times of social and political turmoil are not particularly favorable for sound intellectual or historical judgment. We tend to cultivate and befriend new ideas within a background of safety, once *Clio*, the muse of history, has loosened her grip on our neck. Freud's Vienna epitomized such an era of certitude and introspection that was a fertilizing ground to progressive intellectual movements like psychoanalysis, socialism, Zionism, and expressionism. However, ours is an age of bewilderment and acting out. I doubt if history is holding its breath to see what spiritual treasures, Jewish or psychoanalytic, will come out of the technological frenzy of this age.

So much to the epistemic context of the meeting on the occasion of the annual lecture of Jewish thought and psychoanalysis which informed this volume and from which its spoken words have migrated into print. It is perhaps fitting that I also spell out the emotional context of that meeting in Philadelphia as I perceive it. I rejoiced at the invitation and felt lucky when I realized that my lecture coincided with Freud's birthday. But frankly there is little ground for festivity nowadays for an analyst who is concerned about the future of his discipline in a world that is gradually being run by algorithms. It is even more difficult to sit at my keyboard as an Israeli who is concerned about the future of his country as a liberal democracy. Americans among my readers are shattered by an increase in anti-Semitic assaults in their country. I am pointing this out because even though the first part of my chapter concerns the understanding of past events, I feel that we encounter one another in this work not as dispassionate spectators of bygone historical times but as traumatized witnesses to the making of a new chapter in American, and, possibly, in Jewish, history. I will say more on that in the second part of my text.

Since the early days of psychoanalysis, analysts are indisposed to bring together psychoanalysis with a particular world view (*Weltanschauung*). However, it is hardly possible to understand the dissemination of psychoanalysis and its development in various countries throughout the twentieth century without considering the conflicting intellectual, cultural, and political "climates of opinion" in which psychoanalysis took root. The history of psychoanalysis is thus replete with examples of the relationship between ethnic, sociopolitical, and cultural tensions and the emergence of particular analytic subcultures. This includes, for example, the influence of communism on interpretations of the Oedipus complex in Soviet Russia, the influence of pragmatism on ego-psychology in post-World War II America, or the part played by anti-Americanism in the development of French, and in particular Lacanian, psychoanalysis.

In my book *Freud in Zion: Psychoanalysis and the Making of Modern Jewish Identity* (Rolnik, 2012), I searched for the mental and historical conditions under which the reception of Freud's teachings and the practice of psychoanalysis as therapy became possible in Jewish Palestine/Israel during the first half of the twentieth century. My study hypothesized and laid out the particular set of needs, hopes, and anxieties which made it possible for psychoanalysis to emigrate from Central Europe and flourish in the Jewish society of Palestine. I would like to tease out some of these "elective affinities" between psychoanalysis and modern Hebrew culture and bring them into focus.

How are we to understand the affinity that early Zionists professed to find in Freud's theory?

Zionism's program was, primarily, political, but the movement also encompassed philosophical doctrines, literary writings, and ideas that were more intellectual and theoretical than practically political. Even though it was sometimes viewed as an incarnation of religious ideas or the culmination of a long-term process in Jewish history, Zionist thinking, at the start, was characterized by its pragmatism and its ideological eclecticism. It engaged in an ongoing give and take with dominant ideas of its time that did not have any obvious connection to either nationalism or religious tradition.

In engaging with Darwinism, Nietzscheism, socialism, existentialism, and psychoanalysis, Zionist thinking ranged far and wide across the field of modern science and philosophy. These intellectual movements played an important role in the process of secularization that European Jewish society underwent, and provided (sometimes incompatible) justifications, arguments, and values that were appropriated into the Zionist movement's variegated ideological arsenal. Works by Darwin, Marx, Nietzsche, Spinoza, and Freud were widely discussed and debated within the Jewish community as Zionism was beginning to shape this community's self-understanding.

Zionist discourse deemed especially important those scholarly works that could offer alternatives to the traditional religious explanations for the existential plight of the Jewish people. Translations of Freud's essays into Hebrew, I note in passing, were only second to those of Herzl and Max Nordau in the four decades that preceded the establishment of the Jewish state.

The question of a relationship between Jewish culture (or more diffuse notions of a Jewish "spiritual essence") and the origins of psychoanalysis did not arise only from Sigmund Freud's religious or intellectual upbringing. The polemical tradition that has claimed to diagnose an essentially Jewish element in the mental makeup of the Jews has pervaded European culture for several centuries, and reached its climax at about the same time that Freud began to formulate his ideas on the human mind. The preoccupation with the Jew's body, spirit, and sexuality became, beginning in the second half of the nineteenth century, one of the hottest topics in medicine. Physicians and scientists collated the symptoms and ills unique to the Jews and argued about the causes of the physical and mental distinctiveness of their Jewish patients. Some offered racist, biologistic explanations, while others claimed that the causes were external: social conditions and the low levels of sanitation and nourishment suffered by Jewish communities in Eastern Europe. The scientific-medical discourse on the uniqueness of the Jews drew its inspiration from traditional stereotypes and created new ones. A number of these were then adopted by popular anti-Semitic culture. Some found their way into turn-of-the century chauvinistic and racist philosophies and ideologies; some were adopted by Jewish doctors, who passed them on to their Jewish clients.

Jewish physicians and scholars played an active role in the stigmatization of the Jewish body, and reinforced the myths on which it was based with the demographic and epidemiological data they collected. The dialectic relationship between science on the one hand and myth and ideology on the other played itself out with regard to every one of the Jew's organs and features. His flat feet, hooked nose, scant hair, high forehead, weak eyes, curved spine, nervous stomach, and, of course, his legendary circumcised Jewish penis were all subjects of learned discussion by the best minds. It was argued, for example, that Jews were peculiarly susceptible to hemorrhoids, short-sightedness, and diabetes, but also naturally immune to infectious diseases such as plague, tuberculosis, and cholera—diseases that Jews had been accused of causing from medieval times (Franz Kafka, for instance, associated his tuberculosis with his ethnic identity). The Jew's peculiarity and otherness was stamped on his body. Every physiological or pathological datum was interpreted as a sign of illness and degeneration, or, alternatively, as a mark of exceptional intelligence and sublime spirituality. Jewish doctors stressed the Jewish body's capacity for endurance and survival. They attributed this to Jewish religious customs: circumcision, religiously mandated dietary restrictions, and kosher slaughtering techniques, which were hailed as particularly hygienic. In part, the positive stereotypes, those that ascribed to the Jews, as the People of the Book, exceptional intellectual capabilities, also encouraged Jews to adopt as part of their identities the negative ones about their physical inferiority.

Zionist doctors did not stop with attributing Jewish ailments to a lack of hygiene in the ghettos. They claimed that emancipation and assimilation could not ameliorate the Jewish people's physical illnesses. Arthur Ruppin, the father of Jewish sociology and later one of the shapers of Zionist colonization policy in Palestine, looked at the bio-statistical data and concluded that in fact it was Jews of the upper socioeconomic classes who suffered the most from modern culture. Thus, he argued that, paradoxically, Jews who enjoyed equality and prosperity in the West were plagued by creeping degeneration (Hart, 2000; Gilman, 1993).

Freud's early writings presented a striking contrast to both the established scientific paradigm and the Jewish response to it. With the completion of *Studies on Hysteria* in 1895, explicit rejections of a hereditary conception of neuroses became a regular feature in Freud's papers. In a letter to Wilhelm Fliess in 1897, he declared that he had made it his task to dislodge "the factor of hereditary disposition" in order to shed light on the problem of neurotic illnesses (Brunner, 1991). He argued that the term "degeneration" used by mental health professionals as a major etiologic factor in neurosis implied that there once had been a perfect race whose descendants had gradually deteriorated. Such perfect beings, Freud claimed, had never existed, so it was not proper to call the Jews, or anyone else, "degenerate." By refusing to write as a scientist in a Jewish cause and remaining silent on his own and his patients' Jewish affiliations, Freud departed no less radically from categories used by other Jewish physicians than he did from the dominant paradigm of nervous diseases.

Whenever Freud was asked about the connection between his Jewish origins and his teachings, he made sure not to leave any room for misunderstanding. His analytic and professional identity, he maintained, was completely distinct from his personal and ethnic identity. The only thing he ascribed to his Jewish heritage was his familiarity with the fate of being in the opposition and of being put under the ban of the "compact majority." In his view, it was the historical fate of the Jews, not their racial makeup that made them natural partners in the project of universal psychoanalysis, a project that demanded of its followers free thought, willingness to fight, and an unrelenting quest for the truth.

Like Isaac Deutscher's (1968) "non-Jewish Jews," such as Spinoza, Marx, and Heine, who were able to act simultaneously both from within and without their identity as Jews, Freud stressed the universal imperative that was part and parcel of his Jewish identity. However, he also delimited in his work the "gray area" in which the general concept of identity resides. Freud's Jewish identity, like that of Moses, was essentially incomplete, broken. This fragmented, or hybrid identity, allowed for the fact that individual psychology, like collective psychology, includes a heterogeneous, even contingent set of elements whose origins are outside of the individual human psyche.

Otto Rank, one of Freud's brightest students, pushed the link between Freud's discoveries and Judaism even further: In an essay of 1905, "The Essence of Judaism," Rank stressed the vital role played by Jews in the fight against repression. He argued that the Jews had remained, through their religion, in touch with the repressed, primal element of their psyches. In this they differed from the Gentiles, who had immediately jumped on the bandwagon of culture and civilization. Turning the stereotype of the mental makeup of the Jew on its head, Rank claimed that the Jews possess knowledge of radical treatment of neurosis that sets them apart from all other nations, such that their historical role as psychoanalysts is how to help others recover from their mental illnesses (Rank, 1905). In America Rank will be remembered for his introduction of short-term psychotherapy.

The Zionist revolution understood itself as a total "makeover" of the Jew. Quite a few Zionist thinkers conceptualized the Jewish problem in psychiatric terms, and the field of psychology played a role in replacing Judaism's traditional theological discourse with Zionism's political discourse. An inseparable component of this healing process was the refurbishing of the Jewish mentality. For those who saw Freud's teachings as a call for humans to enter into themselves, to return to the "original" and the "authentic" self, Zionism took on therapeutic meaning. Almost immediately, psychoanalysis found enthusiastic followers among champions of Jewish national particularity. In the new discipline, they found a fusion of radicalism and tradition amenable to their ideological ends. Psychoanalysis was never a *quick fix* solution, but it was nonetheless perceived as a fix to the ailments of secularization.

Moreover, some Freudian texts served as an intellectual arena where the Eastern European and Central European intellectual traditions, with their corresponding Zionist self-understandings, could contend and reconcile. If you read Freud's book *Jokes and Their Relation to the Unconscious* (1905c) you will see that he was steeped in the Eastern European Jewish folklore and culture of his parents.

As early as 1920, Ernest Jones reported to Freud a conversation with Chaim Weizmann, in which the Zionist leader (who would become Israel's first president) took pride in those "poor Galician immigrants who arrive in Palestine with no clothes but holding Marx's *Capital* in one hand and in the other, Freud's *Interpretation of Dreams*" (cited in Rolnik, 2012, p. 43).

Dorian Feigenbaum, the first psychoanalyst to settle in Jerusalem in 1920, was the first soul-doctor in the one and only psychiatric hospital, *Ezrat Nashim*, in Jerusalem that gave serious thought to the extremely high suicide rate among the Jewish pioneers. Feigenbaum rejected the formal explanation given by the Zionist leadership that the suicide cases were merely the result of the dire economic situation and living conditions the newcomers were facing. "The psychoanalyst," Feigenbaum concluded, "was the only witness of the silent battle the Chalutz [Hebrew pioneer] has to fight, not only with malaria and the stony soil, but with an easily comprehensible longing that has been sacrificed to his ideal" (cited in Rolnik, 2012, p. 45).

Freud is known for his rejection of any *Weltanschauung*, be it an ideological or a religious world view, other than the scientific one. But he never tried to step out of history. His private writings bear witness to his interest in world affairs in general and the "Jewish problem" in particular. At the height of the Great War, and in response to the Balfour Declaration of November 1917, Freud wrote to Karl Abraham: "The only thing that gives me any pleasure is the capture of Jerusalem and the British experiment with the chosen people" (ibid., p. 64). The "British experiment" did not enjoy Freud's support for long. In 1930 he wrote to Keren Hayesod: "To me it would have seemed more sensible to establish a Jewish homeland on a historically unencumbered soil [...] Also, I regretfully admit that the unworldly fanaticism of our fellow Jews must bear some responsibility for awakening the mistrust of the Arabs. Nor can I summon up any trace of sympathy for the misguided piety that has made a piece of Herod's wall into a national relic, thereby provoking the natives' feelings" (ibid., p. 68).

Freud's growing skepticism regarding the Zionist project was in part the result of his excavations into Jewish history. His psycho-historical analysis led him to believe that a particular object-relation between the Jews and their ancestral homeland was etched in the mental makeup of the Jews. If psychoanalytic treatment is akin to an exodus from Egypt (as a reading of Freud's 1939 essay *Moses and Monotheism* intimated), then the choice of Palestine as a national homeland for the Jews is akin to a regression to the primordial atavistic strata of Jewish history. "Palestine," he wrote to the writer Arnold Zweig in 1932, "has never produced anything but religious sacred frenzies, presumptuous attempts to overcome the outer world of appearance, by means of the inner world of wishful thinking [...] and it is impossible to say what heritage from this land we have taken over into our blood and nerves ..." (ibid., p. 66).

Unlike Rome or Athens, two ancient cities who happily coexisted in Freud's mind as both real and imagined, Jerusalem was to remain for him a mental topos, a haunted relic from an unrequited past of Jewish history. In 1933 he wrote to Yehuda Magnes, the president of the Hebrew University: "For me, a trip to Jerusalem is perhaps possible from a physical point of view [...] but not from a psychological one" (ibid., p. 64).

In a letter Anna Freud wrote to Max Eitingon, Freud's right-hand man in administrative matters since the early 1920s, who emigrated from Berlin to Jerusalem shortly after Hitler came to power in 1933, she confided to him a dream: "Last night I had a vivid dream of Jerusalem. But it was a mixture of Vienna Forest and Berchtesgaden. It seems that my imagination cannot reach any further then that" (ibid., p. 136). Analytic dispatches of all sorts reached Vienna from Palestine ever since Eitingon and a handful of former Berlin analysts established in 1934 the Palestine Psychoanalytic Society. During the bloody events of the 1936–39 Arab Revolt, a dentist from Berlin, who had recently joined a kibbutz, wrote to inform Freud that some Arab villagers in Palestine were blessed with telepathic powers and that the only method of transmitting information available to the Arabs was by thought transference. Freud cordially thanked the dentist for providing him with further evidence on the subject of telepathy, a secret passion that he was advised to suppress but could never really overcome (ibid., p. 61).

Max Eitingon's report to Freud, written shortly after he established the Palestine Psychoanalytic Society, testified to a determination to not let historical circumstances excessively interfere with the assimilation of Freudian thinking into the Zionist mind: "The intensive building that characterizes this place forces us [analysts] to follow our own private path and not become absorbed too early in public life. After all, it is the same people, with the same problems we had been used to dealing with, as clearly neither orthodox Jews nor Arabs are suitable in any way for psychoanalysis" (ibid., p. 111). The two "Others" of Jewish nationalism—Orthodox Jews and the indigenous Arab population—would be excluded from Israeli psychoanalytic discourse for many years to come. Paradoxically, in the Zionist ideological environment that tended to appropriate the private sphere of the individual for the benefit of the public interest, Freudian psychoanalysis began to offer individual immigrants an instrument to reexamine the borders between inside and out, between their inner world and history. The German-speaking analysts who fled Hitler to Palestine had their hands full.

The formative years of psychoanalysis in Jewish Palestine were shaped by a perpetual tension: While popular psychoanalytic discourse worked ceaselessly toward defusing the social pessimism that was part of Freud's works, it was left for the analysts to safeguard the therapeutic function of psychoanalysis.

That the psychoanalysts of Jerusalem, Haifa, and Tel Aviv could withdraw into their private clinics was of great importance. In his memoir of life in Jerusalem in the 1940s Amos Oz wrote: "The minute you tried to express any private emotion, what always came out was something cramped, arid, even frightened, the product of generations and generations of repression and prohibitions" (2002, p. 15). But withdrawal into the clinic also prevented psychoanalysis from contributing to critical intellectual discourse, where it could have served as an antidote to the proto-messianic rhetoric then prevailing.

Interestingly enough, yet consistent with the reaction of most psychoanalysts at the time, neither the encounter with murderous anti-Semitism nor the imminent Arab–Jewish conflict were openly acknowledged by Freud's followers in Palestine in their scientific and clinical discourse. It was only in the late 1950s that Israeli analysts would gradually acknowledge the Holocaust's direct and indirect effects on the survivors, and on the members of the second generation.

One of the high points in the search by the Israeli Psychoanalytic Society for a way to make a distinctive contribution to the profession took the form of a series of lectures held by the society on the psychological basis of war, in the first half of the 1960s. The result was a book—*The Psychological Bases of War*—that was published two wars later (with the help of the American Friends of the Israel Psychoanalytic Society) and proximate to a third: the Yom Kippur War. The volume's poetic thrust is provided by a foreword written by the transportation minister at the time, young Shimon Peres.

Beginning in the 1960s, and to the present day, Israeli psychoanalysts have published a large number of articles and books devoted to the psychological effects of the Holocaust and on the clinical treatment of survivors and their children and grandchildren. These works consider the implications of the trauma of the Holocaust for Israeli society, the Israeli–Palestinian conflict, and the relations between Israelis and Germans.

Contemporary psychoanalytic discourse in Israel offers still more insights into the relationship between science and ideology, and between political culture and analytic theory. Consider, for instance, the pronounced "trauma-centrism" of the analytic discourse in present-day Israel. The vast majority of younger analysts in Israel today are inclined in their clinical work toward psychoanalytic models of the mind that emphasize the role of actual trauma in mental life. The "imagined patient" of Israeli psychoanalysis seems to be the diametric opposite of the New Man of the Zionist revolution. Whereas the New Man of the Zionist revolution was depicted as someone who freed himself from the shekels of Jewish history and past, the prototypical patient of Israeli psychoanalysis appears to be a fairly passive individual, mostly reactive to his environment and, therefore, hardly accountable to his interiority and his mind. Such analytic theorizing tends to portray the patient as a passive template on which social atrocities or the shortcomings of his significant others are inscribed, rather than as an active agent. It is a trend that has accompanied a steady decline in interest in the dynamic unconscious, in primary aggression, and in promoting the patient's sense of agency and responsibility for both the creative and the destructive forces in his psyche. Clearly, my observations of the development of psychoanalysis in Israel should not be isolated from the overall trend in psychoanalysis in many other countries. One must be careful not to draw simplistic analogies between the political culture of blame that characterizes public life in Israel, and Israel's mental-health community's preferences for psychoanalytic models of the mind that emphasize the impact of environmental calamities on mental functioning. There are, I believe, particular enigmatic messages that are being unconsciously exchanged between the Hebrew-speaking analytic pair that pertain not just to the history of the patient, his unconscious fantasy, or to the subjectivity of the analyst, but also to history at large, that is, to the political and cultural context in which the analytic pair is tapping into the unconscious strata of their encounter. I think Freud would not find this intuition outraging. After all it was he who wrote, in one of his last essays that: "It does not imply any mystical overvaluation of heredity to think it is credible that the psychological peculiarities of families, races, and nations, even in their attitudes toward psychoanalysis, are already laid down for the ego even before it has come into existence" (1937c).

Leaving aside the speculative component of inheritance we are left with a passion for psychoanalysis which is multiply determined, and perhaps reinforced, by a political culture that, on the one hand, seems overly receptive to psychoanalysis as therapy, but, on the other hand, tends to favor the notion that aggression is mainly the result of frustration, or unrequited emotional needs, and that all evil comes from outside.

Zionism has been from its earliest days rife with contradictions, inconsistencies, and dialectical tensions. It offered a new combination of reflective self-observation alongside political action; distinctive, unique, groundbreaking national creation, alongside "normal" existence based on respect for laws and universal values. Zionism was simultaneously rational and romantic, constructivist and interpretative, innovative and vanguard, but it also suffered from the self-celebratory nature of group and ethnic affiliations in ways that hindered its development. It stopped learning from the experience of other nations and began to perceive itself as "one of its kind."

"Some victories are harder to endure than defeats," the historian Jacob Talmon wrote, quoting Nietzsche, in an open letter to Prime Minister Menachem Begin: "Striving to dominate and rule, in the late 20th century, a foreign population that is hostile, different in its language, history, culture, religion, national consciousness and aspirations, in its economy and its social structure, is tantamount to an attempt to revive feudalism," Talmon asserted, in a moving text titled "The Homeland Is in Danger" (published in the newspaper *Haaretz* on March 31, 1980 and included in Talmon, 2015).

Forty years later Israel's military superiority, which makes possible the country's continued existence even in the absence of a political settlement, continues to undermine its democratic, liberal character. Distinguishing between dreams that are worthy of being lived and fought for and pipe dreams, between bold utopian politics and regressive messianic politics, still is the greatest challenge of the Zionist revolution. What, indeed, is it to be an Israeli at this time, if not to dwell within a fragment of yourself, ensuring that the other parts of the picture don't disturb you; to do whatever strikes your fancy and not understand "What's wrong with that?" It is not enough to be aware of the danger that faces Israel from the continuation in power of Prime Minister Benjamin Netanyahu whose policies and way of life embody the Israeli "What's wrong with that?" approach. The touching belief of the "sane Israel" that the flaws of the economy and society and the country's governmental corruption could be redressed without ending Israel's rule over millions of Palestinians and without demarcating permanent borders—is as misguided as the belief of "crazy messianic Israel" that history could be forced to fulfill the prophetic vision and that it is possible to hold on to Greater Israel for all time. There is no right way to lead a life that isn't right.

If Israelis and their friends abroad still retain an iota of utopian political consciousness and love of truth, of the kind that the conceivers of the Zionist dream and the founders of the state and the signers of our Declaration of Independence were endowed with, they must curb those who are threatening to abandon Israel's fate to the forces of gravity of Jewish messianism. As an analyst I would appreciate it if readers let a natural affinity to Israel be informed not just by Jewish solidarity but by a humanistic and analytic love of truth. Every student of Jewish history and culture knows that one need not be on the winning side of history in order to do good.

I expect that working analytically at the frontier of militant nationalism and religious fanaticism is going to be an ever greater challenge for psychoanalysts who seek to enhance their patients' sense of personal agency and encourage them to know themselves in order to be able to think for themselves; to be able to translate historical and personal reality into meaningful psychic experience.

References

Brabant, E., Falzeder, E., & Giampieri-Deutsch, P. (Eds.) (1993). *The Correspondence of Sigmund Freud and Sándor Ferenczi, vol. 1: 1908–1914*. Cambridge, MA: Belknap Press.

Brunner, J. (1991). The (ir)relevance of Freud's Jewish identity to the origins of psychoanalysis. *Psychoanalysis & Contemporary Thought*, 14(4): 655–684.

Deutscher, I. (1968). *The Non-Jewish Jew and Other Essays*. New York: Hill & Wang.

Freud, S. (1912–13). *Totem and Taboo*. Preface to the Hebrew edition. *S. E.*, *13*: 1–161. London: Hogarth.

Freud, S. (1937c). Analysis terminable and interminable. *S. E.*, *23*: 211–253. London: Hogarth.

Gay, P. (1984). *The Bourgeois Experience: Victoria to Freud*. New York: Oxford University Press.

Gilman, S. (1993). *The Case of Sigmund Freud: Medicine and Identity at the Fin de Siècle*. Baltimore, MD: Johns Hopkins University Press.

Hart, M. (2000). *Social Science and the Politics of Modern Jewish Identity*. Stanford, CA: Stanford University Press.

Maltman, A. (2018). *Vineyards, Rocks and Soils*. New York: Oxford University Press.

Oz, A. (2002). *A Tale of Love and Darkness*. London: Chatto & Windus.

Rank, O. (1905). Das Wesen des Judentums. In: D. B. Klein, *Jewish Origins of the Psychoanalytic Movement* (p. 170). Chicago, IL: University of Chicago Press, 1985.

Rolnik, E. J. (2012). *Freud in Zion: Psychoanalysis and the Making of Modern Jewish Identity*. London: Karnac.

Skibell, J. (2002). One street at a time; Vienna's Berggasse. *The New York Times Magazine*, 17 November, https://nytimes.com/2002/11/17/magazine/one-street-at-a-time-vienna-s-berggasse.html (last accessed 24 October 2019).

Talmon, J. B. (2015). The homeland is in danger. In: D. Ohana (Ed.), *Mission and Testimony: Political Essays*. Foreword by Isaiah Berlin. Eastbourne, UK: Sussex Academic Press.

Twain, M. (1899). *Stirring Times in Austria, Literary Essays, vol. 22 of the Writings of Mark Twain*. New York: Harper & Brothers.

Wittels, F. (1924). *Sigmund Freud: His Personality, His Teaching, and His School*. London: Routledge, 2013.

CHAPTER SIX

A Talmudist and a psychoanalyst encounter a Talmud tale

Ruth Calderon and Harvey Schwartz

Introduction

This past year I attended the bat mitzvah of a relative. She gave her speech about the portion of the week and after recounting the Bible narrative she commented, "But on a deeper level ..." She then proceeded to expound on what she understood to be the deeper meanings of the biblical tale. I heard this and I thought to myself—and people wonder why so many Jews become psychoanalysts. An essence of our psychoanalytic work is to be open to, and to invite others to be interested in, significant deeper meanings in what appear to be simply common-sense phenomena. Said succinctly the Freudian essence is to emancipate one's curiosity about our own deeper levels.

This is the similarity between Jewish thought and psychoanalysis—to always consider the deeper levels of meaning. In the 1500s there lived a man in Prague considered by many to be the greatest Jewish scholar, Judah Loew ben Bezalel—more commonly known as the Maharal. He has been credited with the legend of the Golem. One of his great contributions was to emphasize the metaphoric meaning that lay underneath the easily available surface. He wrote in 1598, "The vast majority of the words of the sages are meant in a metaphorical and allegorical way ... therefore, don't be alarmed when you see words which appear foolish and distant from wisdom … they are really hidden messages which are very profound and intelligent" (p. 51). All of us teachers of psychotherapy and psychoanalysis in our own times have said just this to our students. Don't be distracted and misled by the surface—there's more meaning to be gleaned. This is the essential similarity between the psychoanalytic and Judaic world views.

Our joint appreciation of the existence of latent meanings next introduces the question of how we know the accuracy of our suppositions about these latent meanings. Here the two world views separate. In Talmudic study the suppositions about the deeper levels are confirmed by their affiliation with the thinking of prior revered sages and ultimately by their connection to the Torah. In contrast psychoanalytic hypotheses about deeper meanings are either supported or not by here-and-now affective deepening in a patient's experience.

A relatively new patient arrives for his session five minutes late. He proceeds to apologize repeatedly and painfully for this presumed transgression. The analyst could remain on the surface and simply be "nice" to the patient by reassuring him that it is really no big deal and he shouldn't be so hard on himself. Alternatively, interested in deeper meanings, the analyst could invite the patient to be curious about his need to so deferentially present himself to the analyst. The patient may respond by noting that many others in his life have pointed this very character trait out to him and he has noted his inability to stop being so self-effacing even when he realizes it's unnecessary. In fact, he notes that this tendency has impacted his ability to take the initiative both at work and toward his girlfriend with whom he is struggling to be intimate.

These responses from the patient suggest to the analyst that his suppositions are meaningful in the work with this patient. That this patient's excessive apologizing contained deeper meanings was confirmed by his affective associations to the insight. Going to a deeper level, the analyst could consider inviting the patient to be interested in the fact that he likely knew that the traffic is congested at this hour and as they have discussed in the past he could have arranged to leave five minutes earlier. The patient responds by noting that he himself did wonder about his choosing to work up to the very last minute and wasn't surprised that he ended up being late. It brought to his mind a recollection of an unspoken, and presumed to be unspeakable, annoyance that he felt toward the therapist for not being more accommodating to his work schedule.

The point here is that in psychoanalytic work the deeper layers of meaning that the analyst supposes exist within a patient are only confirmed by their emergence in the patient's experience. This deepening of experience allows an individual to become safely familiar with awkward aspects of themselves, especially shame-filled and guilty feelings. When properly done, underlying levels of meaning are not derived from generic theory but through individual experience.

We've noted the similarities—both systems of thought attend to their own versions of deeper meaning. That there are differences between the Judaic and psychoanalytic world views is quite understandable. For one, they each emerge from mindsets separated by 1,500 years. For another, psychoanalysis is a clinical enterprise devoted to uncovering obscured aspects of our minds and personalities in order to free us from repetitive and gratuitous psychic pain. Talmud study is for many to deepen one's exposure to the thinking of those seen as great sages, which is felt as giving access to the divine. Finally, the Talmud is based on the notion of a deity which is seen as informing the truth of its suppositions. In contrast, the psychoanalytic enterprise invites the individual to develop curiosity about the personal meanings that form their particular vision of the divine.

In preparing these words for the introduction to this chapter I had a real-time encounter with both the similarities and differences between these ways of experiencing personal truth. I set out to describe a traditional scholar's approach to Talmud study and I originally wrote, "Talmud study is for many in order to deepen one's exposure to the thinking of those seen as great sages and thereby give access to the divine." That was my understanding of the traditional approach. To be sure about it I asked a traditional Talmud scholar if I was correctly representing his thinking. He wrote me back and corrected what I wrote. By my using the word "thereby" he felt I was incorrectly suggesting that there is a two-step process which implies that the sages are one step removed from the divine.

Psychoanalysts too try to choose their words carefully in order to precisely capture patients' at times elusive unconscious and transferential illusions. The Talmud scholar added, "We would say that in a way, studying their words is studying the divine wisdom." The thoughtfulness and precision bridges our two methodologies. However, the next day the difference was brought into sharp relief. He wrote me, "I would just want to clarify that this is *in no way* implying the sages are the divine" (emphasis included).

To me, this insistent if not anxious carefulness reveals a concern over letting one's mind travel freely. This demonstrates a fundamental difference between the Talmudic and psychoanalytic ideals. The psychoanalytic model says, "Let's know everything about you. Try not to interrupt your imaginings and when you do let's learn about why you feel the need to hesitate. Let's come to appreciate what it is that restricts your thinking, your feeling, your speaking?" Freud actually borrowed from a second century Roman playwright Terence who stated, "Let nothing that is human be alien to me" (163 BC). This is the essence of psychoanalysis. Nothing that is human should be alien. Comedically, this is in contrast to a recent *New Yorker* cartoon where a patient was lying on an analyst's couch with the analyst behind him and the patient says, "Frankly I don't think my intimate feelings are any of my business!"

To return to our patient—there are times in the clinical situation with some patients where an analyst would choose to stay on the surface and straightforwardly offer reassurance. This is similar to what Rav Kahana, who was born in the year 250, said in the Talmud Tractate Shabbat, "When I was 18 years old, I had learned the entire Talmud but I did not know until now that a verse never departs entirely from its surface meaning" (63a). Said more colloquially 1,500 years later—"Sometimes a cigar is just a cigar."

Nowhere is the similarity and differences between these two world views more evident than in their respective approach to dreams.

"A dream that is not interpreted is like a letter that is not read."

This appreciation of the ambiguities, word play, and hidden memories within dreams is the essence of Freud's masterpiece on dreams written in the 1890s. I was startled to learn that the "letter not read" sentence was not written by Freud but in fact was written by Rav Chista who was born in the year 228 and it was published in Tractate Berakhot (55b) of the Talmud.

Freud was very aware of the earlier biblical tradition of dream interpretation and saw his work as an evolutionary extension of it. Though he expressed partiality to the Greek way of thinking about dreams in a letter of 1910, he nevertheless identified himself in his own dreams through the image of Joseph the dream interpreter. Again both the biblical and psychoanalytic models consider the hidden meanings that lie within dreams.

The biblical system from around 580 BC sees the interpretation of dreams as portents of the future. It is the interpreter rather than the dream itself that is considered to be the carrier of the divinely inspired prophetic ability. In contrast, Freud discovered that dreams contain personal meanings. Each dream carries the disguised fingerprint of an individual's unconscious fears and wishes as shaped over the course of his or her life—they illuminate that past rather than foretell the future. In place of their functioning as a vehicle for divinely inspired prophecies or formulaic symbols, psychoanalysis sees the dream as an effort of the deepest parts of our individual souls to be heard.

Rav Chista and the dorshei reshumot—those scholars from the Talmudic period who were interpreters of symbols—and the later Maharal, all long antedated Freud. Despite the differences, they shared with him his essential view of dreams which distinguished them from those who saw dreams as meaningless productions of the brain. Corresponding in 1933, Freud summarized: "In short what according to the opinion of other authors is supposed to be merely an arbitrary improvisation hurriedly brought together in the embarrassment of the moment, this we treat as a holy text" (1900a, p. 514).

There is a bit of prophecy, if you will, in our Jewish past that predicts Freud's dream work. It is not only Joseph who served as the biblical dream interpreter but also Daniel. He in contrast didn't limit his awareness about dreams to just predicting the future. In response to King Nebuchadnezzar who asked him to interpret his dream Daniel said that God gave the dream to him because "He wants you to understand what is in your heart" (Daniel 2:30). This idea of Daniel's that dreams are in fact personal revelations set the stage for Freud two millennia later.

Perhaps this overlap between Jewish and psychoanalytic thinking is best and most simply described by Harold Bloom (1990) when he concluded, "Freud's most Jewish quality was his deep conviction that there is sense in everything, and that such meaning could be brought up to the light. He read the unconscious as Judaic exegesis read the Hebrew Bible, with every nuance, every omission, being made to show an extraordinary wealth of significance."

To give Freud the final word, we will correct an unfortunate mistranslation of the term he coined—psycho-analysis. We Americans understand it to be the combination of analysis, the scientific study of the psyche, the mind. In fact, a proper translation reveals that "psyche" derives from the Greek word for soul, not mind. Indeed Freud set out to enable us to study our souls.

Harvey Schwartz

* * *

Before we start discussing the story together, a few words about myself. I'd like to explain how I first met the classic Jewish texts and how I approach them today. I was raised as a young girl in a Sephardic family. The culture of our family, along with being warm and kind, was very male-dominant. My father and two older brothers were expected to lead the way. My mother—the heart of the family—was loved and appreciated but expected to keep to traditional roles. Growing up, it was a surprise for me that I was expected to take a similar role to my mother's. I was always intrigued by spirituality and narrative. Life in the Israeli secular community was not centered upon the synagogue and ritual. We saw the total Jewish national and secular existence in Israel as the manifestation of our Jewishness. We spoke Hebrew and studied the Bible at school, as well as lived in Hebrew culture rich in Jewish symbolism, values, and esthetics. And yet, Rabbinic Jewish texts, the Mishnah and Talmud, were not part of our intellectual diet. The same was true for Halachic laws.

It was around my bat mitzvah, at the age of twelve, that I felt there was something missing. In the very vivid culture of the young state of Israel, I missed the depth and gravitas of the Jewish canon. I began searching for a place where I could study the classic texts. Everywhere I looked, I was expected to change my affiliation as a prerequisite.

As much as I longed for the "missing link" in my Jewish identity, I had no intention of turning my back on the community and family that raised me and their Jewish way. And I was searching for my own path. When I entered the world of study, it felt as though we were reading God's diary. There was something very personal and intimate about it for me. I found the Talmud to be a source of wisdom, humor, and relevance to my life.

Midrash, one of the rabbis' main intellectual tools, intrigued me in its ability to help me study ancient classic text, and to find its relevance to life today in a way that is both accurate and creative. My metaphor for Midrash is that of a kite. When you want to fly a kite, you must tightly hold on to the string and at the same time, give it plenty of freedom to let the kite soar in the sky. If you hold the string too close or too short, it won't fly. The string that you hold is the text: the word or the sentence from the Bible. And the kite dancing in the air is your new creative interpretation that you will think about today. If you let go of the string it will just be paper and wind and it won't be an interpretation. It will fly away. If you don't let it fly high, and hold it tight with the string, it won't be a kite. It will not be able to fly. There needs to be tension between the string you are holding and the kite going free in the sky. The freedom of the kite flying allows you to go beyond where you imagined it would be able to go. Like with good Midrash, holding tight gives freedom.

The creators of the Talmudic stories were a small group of thinkers. I see them as somewhat similar to Buddhist monks, living in a tight community, creating miniature, sophisticated stories. These stories seem to me as works of art, and their aim was to awaken awareness and make their human and religious life a richer one.

Those storytellers are part of a generation that revolutionized the way Jews saw themselves in contrast to the Temple Jewish culture centered in Jerusalem. They developed a modular Judaism that could be practiced anywhere in the world. Instead of sacrificing animals they developed prayer and study as ways of worship. Instead of the priest being born to be the ideal type, they invented the new ideal type which was themselves: the rabbi, the scholar.

To be a scholar is a life journey. It's a journey that involves constant study—of text and of life situations. There's a belief that the text is waiting for you personally and that God hid a little note with your name on it in the text. If you don't look for this special wisdom that was put there for you, this wisdom will be lost. This involves a sense of responsibility. It might take years, but one might go back to the same text again and again. In the Kabbalah there is the image of wooing a beautiful woman. Though I'm not traditionally religious I do believe that the study of classic texts enables us to find new meaning that was not yet understood. Perhaps in that way it is like psychoanalysis.

The rabbis' way of life at the time is important for the story we're going to read together. In Babylon they developed the concept of the Yeshiva. The best young men were selected to be educated in the Yeshiva and later would become the communities' spiritual leaders. These rabbis would marry at a young age, but leave their home and wives for the Yeshiva for most of the year. The wives had pivotal roles in some of the stories, although they are secondary characters and anonymous. In Aramaic [the language of the Talmud] the word for wife is "home." They say that without a wife a man is homeless.

The Talmud is not feminist, is not democratic, and is not liberal. It is a sometimes chauvinist, ancient, male-centered Jewish classic text. That said, it is mine. I love, respect, and am loyal to it while at the same time I feel free to criticize and hold different views. Further, what I do when I find a real, seriously upsetting piece of the Talmud, is that I stop. I read it as a rabbi. I identify in these stories with a rabbi because these are stories that were written by rabbis for rabbis and if I want to read well, I need to read it as the hero of the story. Not as the support actress that is going to get hurt, because I'm not a support actress. In my life, I am the protagonist.

I'm inviting you today also, at least as an option, to read the story as the rabbi. This story is one that I wrote in relation to a piece of the Talmud. The story that I wrote is my kite. I let my imagination go as far as it could as long as I hold on to the text. I let my kite fly high.

Ruth Calderon

* * *

A Bride for One Night by Ruth Calderon*

When Rav would visit the city of Darshish, he would announce: "Who will be mine for a day?"

And when Rav Nachman would visit the city of Shachnetziv, he would announce, "Who will be mine for a day?"

B. Yoma 18b

When Rav would visit Darshish once or twice a year, the whole syna-gogue would get caught up in a frenzy of excitement and Rav would lock himself up for hours in this study house to settle matters of law that had been left unresolved. On Shabbat he would come to pray in the synagogue at the top of the hill which looked out on the whole town and its houses,

*Reproduced from *A Bride for One Night* by Ruth Calderon, translated by Ilana Kurshan, by permis-sion of the University of Nebraska Press. English translation copyright 2014 by the Deborah Harris Agency. Originally published as Hashuk, Habayit, Halev, copyright 2001 by Ruth Calderon.

yards, orchards, and gardens. Through the screen marking off the women's section I could see him standing before the ark to lead the congregation in prayer. His body was erect, his form splendid in a robe of fine stitching, and his bright forehead unblemished by sun, and all the men clustered around him as if he were a prince.

On laundry days among the women I heard rumors that they were looking for someone to serve as Rav's wife for the duration of his visit to our town. And so when the synagogue beadle sought me out in my backyard four weeks prior to Rav's visit, I knew what he had come to say. He found me with my sleeves rolled up and my hands buried in a basket of laundry delighting in the pleasant odor of clean clothes and the warm sun that would dry them all. I was not a young woman anymore. Eight years had passed since I had been widowed.

At first, I let the beadle stammer in embarrassment about the role they needed me to play and hint at the assistance I would receive from the community and the amount of ketubah money I would be paid if the rabbi should elect to divorce me after the fact. I requested some time to think over the matter and I sent the man on his way. While lying in bed that night I resolved that I would accede—because of the money and because of what people always say: "Two is better than one." And because it had been years since I had known the feel of the man's caress and the smell of his breath, and I yearned for those days again.

The next day when the beadle returned, I nonetheless gave him a hard time before agreeing to his terms lest I seem overly eager. He conveyed a few strictures that I had to be sure to keep so that I would be ritually pure in advance of the rabbi's visit. His concern that I might begin to bleed as a result of excitement and anticipation seemed rather excessive if not downright amusing. Nonetheless, I carefully calculated the days of my menstrual cycle as if I were a young bride. They would open the ritual bath especially for me in the darkness of night so that no one would see me.

The days raced by. On the eve of the rabbi's arrival word spread that he had permitted the remarriage of two "chained widows," women who have lost their husbands in a recent flood. A wave of grateful approval washed over the community and even I was enchanted by the news. As the rabbi stood at the head of the synagogue giving his talk, his wandering gaze rested on me for a moment. Along with the rest of the community I felt drawn to his visage. From my place among the women I felt as if my mourning clothes and kerchief were blushing. A forgotten feeling awoke inside me. I wanted to get closer to him.

During the reception that followed his talk, Rav was surrounded by a crowd that sought his blessing and kissed the palms of his great hands. The leaders of the community allowed him a brief respite from the crowd and on the terrace of the synagogue amid a great sea of people I stood there before him.

I heard him turn to the surrounding men and ask, "Who will be my wife for today?" Perhaps I didn't exactly hear him say that, but I read his intentions in the curl of his lip and I knew that I was not the only one who heard the question: virgins hid their faces and mothers pulled their curious daughters outside and away. There were already a few women who were known to have spent the night with Rav on one of his previous visits. Two of them had come to the synagogue dressed in full finery. Strutting to and fro. One of them even looked Rav in the eye and gave him a knowing smile. He nodded back to her in blessing.

I walked toward him with lowered eyes, my feet padded against the floor to the rhythm of my fluttering heart. I approached no farther than honor would permit. The beadle whispered in his ear as Rav looked in my direction and gestured to me to come closer.

A murmur passed over the crowd and I felt suddenly relieved that my elderly mother had stayed at home. I thought about the chatter of the local kitchen maids who dice up gossip into bite-sized morsels. I feared for my good name as I raised my eyes. Rav's face was luminous and shone only on me. His beadle approached and led me out of the crowd and into a new reality. A door was opened to a side room, Rav disappeared and the crowd began to slowly disperse. I stood there as if paralyzed. I heard from a distance the instructions of the beadle in my ears. "When it gets dark … in the town inn … in the great guest room … there His Honor will await you."

I had become a bride for a moment, even that old feeling of embarrassment seized me as if I were a virgin. When I rushed home, the sun had already sunk to the height of the trees. I moved about the house silently, washed my face in cold water, dressed in a clean frock and walked out into the empty streets with wet hair amid the melodies of the evening prayers. The light of the oil lamps dancing in the windows spilled out into the street which had become my wedding canopy.

Rav was immersed in solitary study in the corner of the room. I was greeted by his beadle, a man I found not particularly pleasant. I kept my distance. Suddenly the rabbi of the town appeared with two witnesses. I stood there as if dreaming with Rav at my side, my head reaching only to the height of his chest. There was no wedding canopy and no candles but I heard once again the words of the wedding blessing. "Who forbids to us … and permits to us … by means of the canopy and sanctification." The words were spoken like an ordinary prayer, quickly, unaccompanied by the tears of my smiling parents. Rav said in his stentorian voice, "Behold, you are sanctified unto me," and handed me a handkerchief from his pocket. I reached out my hand and took it. The rabbi and his attendants checked that the handkerchief had been properly transferred and muttered in approval. Rav said to them, "You are my witnesses." And the rabbi concluded, "She is sanctified." And then everyone left the room as if they had never been there.

Then there was just the two of us, he and I in the guest room of the town inn. It was our wedding canopy, and our bedroom, and our house, and our whole world for one night. Rav did not mince words and did not try to win me over as young men are wont. He also didn't fall all over me—he just sat by my side. I could see his eyelashes which were long and straight as he is. He looked at me with curiosity and with a certain tranquility and I returned his gaze. The look of his face appealed to me even more from up close and I delighted in him like a young girl. The room and the honor of the man who sat crossed legged beside me seemed to me like all I would want of heaven. My life, exhausted and well-worn like a paved road, had suddenly led me to a main thoroughfare that I never expected to traverse. The heads of the community, the luminaries of a generation, and me.

Rav began to say a few words about the town and we sat for an easy hour exchanging pleasantries until I nearly forgot the whole reason that I entered into this hasty matrimony. Suddenly, he took my hand in his and brought it to his mouth. My breath fled, then fluttered and relaxed like a dove. His eyes gazed upon me as if I were a vision. I realized then that I had found favor in his eyes. With the shedding of gowns and scarves, names and roles and titles fell away. He became a man. And I cast off my widowhood and became once again a woman. Our nakedness opened the floodgates of our hearts and there was nothing to worry about and no reputation to uphold. After all, this man was no villain and was not the rabbi responsible for it all?

His body in its full expanse was mine by right and holy law and there was no fear that our union was "not for the sake of heaven," as our teachers used to warn us about in school. I delighted in the sound of the word "my husband" which served as an invitation and a request; it brought back the old sense of being conquered in want. Our bodies did not know if palm would fit to palm, if hip to hip. We had been taught the proper way of touching on this day but I was not the young bride I had once been, nor was I the woman I had been the day before. And this man was at once far and close, as if he were always a part of me, passing through me like a shadow; and I tasted of his goodness and I smelled him and touched him and felt my own fingers come alive and went into him and took himself inside me, and I built up and knocked down and draped myself around him and relished the full surrender that had never been so complete; and my hunger for his breath and for the scent of his body could not be satisfied; and his body was hot and steamy until it reached complete rest.

We were splayed across the bed when I opened my eyes, my body full and I saw that he was looking at me. "I'll take you with me," he said. "Come home with me, my wife." I smiled and kissed his forehead and fell back to sleep. In the morning he continued to sleep after I had awoken. It is commonly believed that larger bodies require more rest. I woke up and looked at him as if he were a dream that had not vanished with the passage of night. I banished all thoughts of a baby with a face like Rav and all thoughts of following him back to his home. Once again, he did not seem like the great Rav. The form of his body was known to me, like that of a little boy whose fears I had assuaged. I knew what I would do. I put on my frock and I dropped his handkerchief over the bed, drawing its smell once more toward me—and it drifted to the bed wondrously and simply, just like our marriage.

* * *

RC: I wrote this story to give voice to women who are so often silent and to try to tell the story from her perspective. This text from the Talmud is not even a story. It's a historical note. This is what rabbis would sometimes do when they traveled. They would marry someone for the night and then they would divorce them. It doesn't sound very nice—what were they thinking? And what were the women thinking? Why would a woman agree to marry someone and then get divorced? Reading it, I thought: If it were me, why would I agree? And then I thought: What if this was an egalitarian option? You go to a conference somewhere, you marry someone, you have a nice weekend, and then you go back home. Definitely a different view on the rabbis.

HS: My challenge is to present a psychoanalytic point of view about this story. The best way I came up with was to imagine if each one of the characters of the story in turn came to my office for a consultation. When I read the story and was trying to get to know Rav I found myself thinking of a patient who in fact came to see me years ago, which I will mention, of course well disguised. This was a man in his thirties who had a life in many ways similar to that of Rav. He too traveled the country making presentations. He was a charismatic man who had followers wherever he went. One might consider that had he been in the entertainment world they would have been called "groupies." For example, after he completed his public presentation he would go out to his car and there would be women in it waiting for him.

It was during this time that he came to me because he was unhappy with his life. He described his sexual adventures and over time came to recognize that the women he bedded had neither interest nor affection for him. They seemed to enjoy being associated with celebrity and he enjoyed having his need for adoration satisfied. With further reflection and honesty he recognized that he had neither interest nor affection for them either. Once he recognized his own neediness he discovered something else in him that sexual excitement screened. He came to discover his secreted and long-standing loneliness. This led him to recall his childhood which he had never thought much about. He immediately started speaking of his sense of alienation from his father. This then led to his recognition of how fragile he felt his masculinity to be. Despite his outward appearances to the contrary he continued to experience himself as a frightened little boy. The remedy he unconsciously sought was to aggressively possess as many women as he could in an attempt to shore up this fragility. It also was an effort to prove to his father that he didn't need him in order to be a man. Over time he became able to center himself without adulations and hypersexuality and married a loving woman. He also changed professions.

With that in mind, I pictured Rav coming to my office and telling me that he too is unsatisfied in his life. He would tell me that he travels far and wide and is practically worshipped by his admirers. "They turn over to me all their personal problems and they ask me for magical solutions. I provide these solutions and strangely they seem satisfied. I make a living and get respect but I am left bewildered that these people imagine that I know what is better for them than they are able to figure out for themselves. In truth this is getting old for me. My satisfying their need to put me on a pedestal is proving to no longer be gratifying. In truth the women I 'marry for a night' ask so little from me. I feel like a prop in their need for a celebrity. In fact, despite this stature that they assign me, I'm afraid of my wife. I'm afraid to tell her how lonely I am. I'm afraid to tell her that I miss intimacy with her. I'm afraid to tell her that I'm afraid to tell her. I'm afraid she'll yell at me. Yes, I know when I was little my mother was a yeller, but for now it's my wife that I'm afraid of. There must be more for me in this life."

He continues, "Perhaps if you and I work together you can help me learn to be other than a great man in other people's eyes but rather a capable man in my own eyes. I can learn how to treat others with dignity. I can also learn to listen to my heart and my hurts and learn how to share them with my wife. Do you think we can accomplish this?"

RC: My first thought is that Rav was so famous that he was simply called Rav (Rabbi, The Master). He was one of the first rabbis and his name was Abba Arikha. He was a tall and beautiful man. He indeed was a widely revered man considered one of the greatest sages of his time. My second thought is about the woman. In a traditional society where men have all the power, it could be understood that an unmarried woman could gain from such a connection. Further, unlike your charismatic patient, Rav is both a man and Torah. His charisma in my view doesn't derive only from his personality but also from his ownership of something that is bigger than him. When people adore him, it's not really only him they adore, but also the Torah that he represents.

I think about the loneliness of people that are on the road. Everyone thinks that life is grand for them but they end up in the motel by themselves doing their laundry alone.

HS: When Ruth and I discussed our conversation earlier, we hoped that we would find areas of disagreement—it makes for a more thought-provoking encounter. I think we just hit upon one of those disagreements. It was your saying that he is not only himself but he has charisma because he has Torah. All of us who work in clinical fields have seen those who possess socially valued grandeur. They are not any less lonely, conflicted, or sad than the poorest of the people we see. Having great knowledge, great wealth, great beauty doesn't spare us. However, one of the burdens of outward success as demonstrated in your story with Rav is that people relate to them as things—things that they try to get close to in order to feel what they imagine is their light cast upon them. These "celebrities" are not seen or known for who they actually are but for what they can bring to those who seek them out. He may be affiliated with Torah. That does not make him any more or less a lonely person. At the end of the day he is someone who is left to seek warmth from strangers. Allegorically Torah may be described as the source of light. Human warmth, necessary for us all, comes from human intimacy. His mastery of Torah doesn't change his essence as a person, a man, a lonely man. As you characterize him he is someone who appears to be hesitant to speak with and be loyal to his wife. In the end of your tale you reveal him to be as a boy, a lonely boy.

RC: I would add to that. Because he is a rabbi and the head of a yeshiva, he is a loyal person. He was famous for teaching his students that you shouldn't behave toward another person as if they were an object. Now he is going to marry someone in order to not be alone, which of course is objectifying her. In order to justify his deed, he marries her. The fact that it worked in that world is somewhere between horrifying and funny.

How does the woman come to you?

HS: The woman comes to my office and says, "You can tell by how I'm dressed that I'm a widow. Perhaps you can tell by how weary I am that I've been a widow for a long time. I'm here because something happened last night that I need to better understand. I had a dream. There's something important in this dream that I'd like to talk to you about. In this dream I was chosen. My whole life I've struggled to be chosen. I have two sisters and I never was the one chosen. But in my dream, I was chosen! I was chosen by the grandest person one could be chosen by—a great rabbi. It was lovely. It felt like I went back in time and that I was a young girl. It felt like I imagine heaven to be. I even felt as if I was a virgin again. But I guess I did feel guilty, maybe as I did as a youngster as well. For even in the dream I had to make up a silly marriage ceremony to make our meeting OK. Not only that but I felt relieved that my mother wasn't there. Imagine, a woman of my age still concerned about my mother knowing about my sexuality.

"So, he and I 'married for the night.' And as dreams would have it, it was wonderful lovemaking. I haven't been with a man in forever and it was perfect—like hand in glove. And then something different happened. Have you ever had a dream within a dream? When you're dreaming but even in the dream you know that you are dreaming.

"That's what happened. He and I were together in the middle of the night. Then I started becoming aware that this was a dream. And that it wasn't really the answer to my real life. He actually asked me to come home with him. Can you imagine me along with his wife? But since it was my own dream, my creation, perhaps the neediness that I had represented in him was in reality a reflection of my own neediness. Perhaps there was a part of me that wanted to stay in the fairyland world where I was chosen and all was wonderful. But enough of me knew that being married to this magical creation was just a dream and that in fact there is real life to contend with. So, I got up and left this make-believe marriage behind. But the dream was in my mind to teach me something and that's why I'm here. The dream spoke to me of my passions that have for so long been buried. I now recognize that I do wish to get married. Not to a dream-like celebrity but to a real present and caring man. Someone who will wish to and be able to know me. Someone who is available to be with me, to choose me. Not as if I were a child but as two adults making their way together in this real life.

"I'm hoping that I can use the energy from this dream to help me build this life with someone.

"Can you help me with that?"

RC: I see this woman as a very down-to-earth person. When women are in a male-dominated society they need money and freedom. In the Greek world, if a woman was widowed, she couldn't own anything. She had to go back to her father or her brother to live under their protection. In the Jewish community of the rabbis, a woman could own things for herself. We know that because Roman matrons would come to live with the Jews where they could keep their status and money. I see her as being very practical and unsentimental.

She is willing to sleep with this rabbi and even compete for the role of wife because she might earn a stipend and status. Afterwards, had he just left her I imagine she would have wanted him more. But when he mentioned the option of her coming back with him as a second wife, it didn't appeal to her. When he said he wanted her to come home with him, he lost his allure. Once he said that, she could let go. She just left him a sort of transitional object, her handkerchief.

HS: You might wonder so who's the next character to walk into the office? It's the beadle. The beadle comes in and says, "You probably don't know who I am. That's because nobody knows who I am. In fact, nobody who ever heard this story would ever think I'd be a character in it. But you know, I'm a person too. And I may be the last one to know that. You see, the reason I'm here is that nobody knows who I am. I'm a bit player. I've never been a lead actor ever.

"You analysts may have something when you say that childhood impacts adulthood. When I was a kid, my parents divorced. All I ever wanted from them is that they get back together. Look what I do for a living now, I put people back together. It didn't work with my parents; I don't know how well it's working for me now either. But I want something else for myself. I don't want to be the bit player; I don't want to be the one who arranges other people having lives. I want to get my own life.

"But there are a few problems with that. These women, I don't understand them at all. Their bodies, their bleeding, their excitement, it confuses me. To tell you the truth, I don't even know so much about my own body. Secretions, dreams—you see, I've never been with a woman. I've been so busy taking care of other people being together, I've never been with a woman. I've never been anything more than a bit player. Check out that woman's dream, I barely appeared in it. So I'm here to become a person. Become a protagonist in my own life. What do you think? Can you help me do that?"

RC: You surprised me when you brought up the beadle, because I wasn't aware of his role as a protagonist.

HS: That's the point, nobody is.

RC: The beadle is a fixer. You made the beadle a more rounded character.

[Question from the audience] What do you imagine Rav's wife was like?

HS: I did picture her coming to the office and I had a few different versions come to mind. First, I imagined her coming in and saying, "I just found out what my husband's been doing on his travels." From there, one could go lots of different places. She could say, "I'm done, I want out. I want you to help me separate from this man." That's one way she could present. Alternatively, she could come in and say, "You know, I've actually realized I've known about his other 'marriages' forever. I don't know what's to be for us, but I do have to look at myself, because truth be told, I've been a cold wife for the past few years. We haven't been intimate; we haven't been warm with each other. I made it very difficult for him to find a welcome home here. Maybe we can work it out, maybe we can't, but maybe I should take a look at myself too."

References

Bezalel, ben, Judah Loew (1598). Be'er HaGolah, p. 51.

Bloom, H. (1990). Foreword. In: Frieden, K., *Freud's Dream of Interpretation*. Albany, NY: State University of New York Press.

Freud, S. (1900a). *The Interpretation of Dreams. S. E.*, 4–5: 514. London: Hogarth.

Freud, S. (1910, October 3). Letter to Alter Druyanov. Freud Museum, London.

Terence (163 BC). "Homo sum, humani nihil a me alienumputo." In: *HeautonTimorumenos* [play].

Index